M000204814

prayfully

"In *Pray Fully*, Michele Faehnle and Emily Jaminet do a wonderful job in helping women who want to pray. Drawing from their experiences as busy moms and wives as well as from work and ministry, they are able to provide tried-and-true advice to help readers grow in intimacy with Jesus. They are honest, authentic, and wonderful examples of women who struggle to grow closer to God but continue to persevere in grace."

Rev. Dave Pivonka, T.O.R.
President of Franciscan University of Steubenville

"*Pray without ceasing; continual prayer; make your work your prayer.* Most of us have heard spiritual directors, the saints, scriptures, and the *Catechism* exhort us to these practices. But what does it really mean and look like for so many of us in the trenches of our family's chaotic daily schedules? *Pray Fully* is a book in which Michele Faehnle and Emily Jaminet hope to equip us to start making these disciplines our own, day by day, in order to find joy again in our lives."

Becky Carter
Host of *Thriving in the Trenches* podcast

"Prayer is a beautiful adventure and journey. It is even better when we have the opportunity to travel with people who 'get it.' While reading *Pray Fully*, I felt like Michele Faehnle and Emily Jaminet were close friends traveling with me. I very much enjoyed and appreciated their personal experiences of prayer, and I think you will love the way that they illustrate prayer and offer practical steps and opportunities to journal and reflect. If you read this book and follow the steps you will find yourself growing in prayer like never before and experience deeply the personal love of God—the Father, Son, and Holy Spirit."

Rev. Michael Denk
Author of *Pray 40 Days*

"Prayer is as necessary for the Christian life as oxygen is for human life. Every vocation requires a mature prayer life. Michele Faehnle and Emily Jaminet provide an amazing reflection for every daughter of the Father to grow and mature as a woman of prayer. Faithful to the wisdom of the Church and her saints and devotions, Faehnle and Jaminet give practical direction for women to progress in prayer and to make it a priority in the lives of their families."

Rev. Adam Streitenberger
Bishop's Coordinator for Evangelization
Diocese of Columbus

"*Pray Fully* leads the reader with the simplest and most profound steps to find a personal way to talk to Jesus and hope for his answer. I have been at prayer in the abbey for more than fifty years, and this is a book on prayer I would recommend to anyone, from eight to eighty."

Mother Dolores Hart, O.S.B.
Author of *The Ear of the Heart*

"This book touched my heart and soul in a way that drew me deeper into the love and power of God. The thought-provoking reflections and questions for journaling are prayers in themselves, and the real-life journeys of Emily Jaminet, Michele Faehnle, and the saints show us the simple yet profound way to grow closer to our Lord and each other and to grow in a life of holiness to touch the world around us."

Lisa Morris
President of Sacred Heart Apostolate
Columbus, Ohio

"I love this book! It is practical, easy to read, and vibrant with rich teaching from the Church's tradition. They have struck a perfect balance that will invigorate the hearts of those who read it!"

Rev. Nathan Cromly, C.S.J.
President of the Saint John Institute

prayfully

Simple Steps for Becoming a woman of prayer

Michele Faehnle   Emily Jaminet

AVE MARIA PRESS AVE Notre Dame, Indiana

Scripture texts in this work are taken from the *New American Bible, Revised Edition* © 2010, 1991, 1986, 1970 Confraternity of Christian Doctrine, Washington, DC, and are used by permission of the copyright owner. All rights reserved. No part of the *New American Bible* may be reproduced in any form without permission in writing from the copyright owner.

Further permissions acknowledgments are found on page 119.

© 2020 by Michele Faehnle and Emily Jaminet

All rights reserved. No part of this book may be used or reproduced in any manner whatsoever, except in the case of reprints in the context of reviews, without written permission from Ave Maria Press®, Inc., P.O. Box 428, Notre Dame, IN 46556, 1-800-282-1865.

Founded in 1865, Ave Maria Press is a ministry of the United States Province of Holy Cross.

www.avemariapress.com

Paperback: ISBN-13 978-1-59471-973-8

E-book: ISBN-13 978-1-59471-974-5

Cover image © gettyimages.com.

Cover and text design by Katherine Robinson.

Printed and bound in the United States of America.

Library of Congress Cataloging-in-Publication Data
Names: Faehnle, Michele, author. | Jaminet, Emily, author.
Title: Pray fully : simple steps for becoming a woman of prayer / Michele Faehnle and Emily Jaminet.
Description: Notre Dame, IN : Ave Maria Press, 2020. | Includes bibliographical references. | Summary: "In Pray Fully the bestselling authors of Divine Mercy for Moms, Michele Faehnle and Emily Jaminet, share the rewards and frustrations of their own prayer journeys to create a practical prayer guide that combines testimonies, tips, and journaling space to help the reader spend quality time with God."-- Provided by publisher.
Identifiers: LCCN 2019046637 (print) | LCCN 2019046638 (ebook) | ISBN 9781594719738 (paperback) | ISBN 9781594719745 (ebook)
Subjects: LCSH: Prayer--Catholic Church. | Prayer--Christianity. | Catholic women--Religious life. | Christian women--Religious life.
Classification: LCC BV215 .F34 2020 (print) | LCC BV215 (ebook) | DDC 248.3/2082--dc23
LC record available at https://lccn.loc.gov/2019046637
LC ebook record available at https://lccn.loc.gov/2019046638

To our mothers,

Jackie and JoAnn,

who taught us to become women of prayer,

and our daughters,

Mary Kate,

Juliana, Leah,

Catherine,

Mary, and Elizabeth,

may we inspire you

to pray fully!

Contents

INTRODUCTION

Why Is Prayer Important?

Michele's Story

"Time to pray the Rosary!"

This was a familiar phrase in my childhood home. It was often met with eye rolling, complaining, and excuses from me and my seven siblings. After experiencing a deep conversion while I was in second grade, my parents began leading us in a family Rosary every day during Lent, a practice that they continue to this day. As their faith continued to deepen and grow, over the years I was exposed to many types of prayer. We went to daily Mass and eucharistic adoration, offered the Chaplet of Divine Mercy, and belonged to a charismatic prayer group.

And yet, although I had been given every opportunity to learn to pray as a child, I didn't really grasp the fullness of what prayer was until I was an adult. Up until that time, my communications with God were mainly rote prayers coupled with petitions (asking God for what I needed and hoping he would grant my requests). To me, God was like a heavenly vending machine, and I only talked to him when I needed something—putting in my Our Fathers, Hail Marys, and Glory Bes and waiting for the magic to happen.

Once I left home, and my faith life began to mature, I came to realize that prayer is actually about having a relationship with God. As I learned to stop making demands of God and simply rest in silence, I began to hear God calling me and beckoning me to draw closer to him. Building this relationship has taken time, but as I have sought to connect to God in prayer, things have changed. I no longer feel like a bratty teenager only going to a parent when I need something. Now that relationship is based on love.

The thing is, many Catholics have never taken the next step in their prayer journey. Fr. Michael Denk writes, "Many of us do go our entire lives praying like we were taught in the second grade. What you learned was not wrong, but have you grown? Has your prayer life deepened and evolved each and every day, week and month since second grade? If not, you might be spiritually out of shape, spiritually dead."[1]

The purpose of prayer is to lead us to God. Prayer is the calling for us to interact with God our Creator on a personal and intimate level. St. John Chrysostom said, "Whether or not our prayer is heard depends not on the number of words, but on the fervor of our souls" (CCC, 2700). When we pray, we quiet our minds and allow God the opportunity to speak to our hearts and instruct us. When we hear God's voice, we can know his will for our lives—and pray in order to conform our own will to his.

Are you in the 51 percent?

According to a report by the Center for Applied Research in the Apostolate (CARA), only 51 percent of Catholic women surveyed pray daily (barely half!).[2] Why is that? Yes, it can be difficult to carve out time with God, and to learn to pray. On the other hand, prayer cannot be something we leave on the back burner and only pull out in times of need. Prayer is the lifeblood of our faith, a two-way conversation with God that alternately comforts, strengthens, and inspires.

We understand that we should be praying always, but when Catholic women who reported they prayed at least occasionally were asked when they pray, the overwhelming majority (80 percent) shared the reason they turned to God "most of the time or always" was during periods of crisis. Is it any wonder, then, that we sometimes have difficulty feeling God's presence in our daily lives? God wants to be our refuge, a stronghold where we can be spiritually refreshed. However, we cannot wait until crisis hits to begin the relationship. When storms strike our lives, if our prayer life is underdeveloped we can easily be swept away, crushed by the circumstances.

Why do you struggle?

As we began to research this topic, we asked women what they struggled with when trying to grow in their prayer life. Here are some of their responses. Do you recognize yourself in any of these?

- "I'm a cradle Catholic. I have a hard time doing anything but memorized prayers."
- "I feel silly trying to make up prayers myself."
- "I'm not sure how to get started or keep it going."
- "My mind starts to wander as I am speaking to God."
- "I just don't have time to pray."

These are all very real and understandable barriers to growing in our prayer life and in our relationship with God. Prayer is a grace and a gift, but it requires effort. Much like diet and exercise, it takes time and dedication. "Prayer cannot be reduced to the spontaneous outpouring of interior impulse: in order to pray, one must have the will to pray. Nor is it enough to know what the Scriptures reveal about prayer: one must also learn how to pray" (CCC, 2650).

The good news is that God longs for you to come to him. God loves you and tirelessly calls you into deeper relationship with him through prayer. It is my great hope that through the pages of this book you will be inspired to cultivate the daily

habit of prayer, and find the courage to approach God—both
to tell him your deepest thoughts and to listen to what he has
to say to you. As you take these first steps in daily prayer,
remember that God delights even in our baby steps to get to
know him. Take that first step—and see how God responds!

Emily's Story

Like Michele, I was raised in a Catholic home with many
opportunities to pray, but it wasn't until I was well into my
twenties that I realized the necessity of a deep prayer life.

For a long time, my prayer life was anemic; the only time
I gave to God was Sunday Mass, prayer before meals, bedtime
prayers with my children, and the occasional, "Please help
me, God!" My brother, Fr. Jonathan Wilson, was always gently
nudging me to make prayer a priority, but I kept pushing it
off, thinking I'd have time "later." Before long, my soul was
"running on empty"; it was like trying to drive a sports car
without any gas. I was trying to run my life and do God's will
without being plugged in to him.

Learning to pray like the saints

When I started reading about the lives of the saints for inspiration, I knew that I needed to make a change. These holy men
and women fueled their lives with prayer. They spent several
hours each day in prayer—attending daily Mass, saying the
Rosary, praying the Liturgy of the Hours, and often going to
adoration.

How did they find the time for all that? Most of them
had personal responsibilities to family and community. Yet
the saints learned to combine work with continual prayer and
even contemplation, and by their example we can learn to do
the same, prayerfully attending to our duties.

Reading about the lives of the saints, I discovered that prayer provides the strength we need to serve and care for those around us. Prayer is our daily fuel, despite how difficult it can be to find the time to pray. I have learned over the years the truth of the saying "you cannot give what you do not have." Without prayer, it is all too easy to become mired in our daily routine and lose our eternal perspective.

At the same time, my prayer life must reflect my vocation as a laywoman as well as my particular stage in life. I must resist the temptation to resent those duties that are an integral part of my calling. If the saints could learn from Christ himself to combine their work with continual prayer, we can be inspired to do the same with our duties, turning even the most mundane task into a kind of prayer. While praying in this way may not be a substitute for quiet, contemplative prayer, it still has value in the eyes of God.

The art of living "pray-fully"

As a working mother of seven children, I at times would prefer to be immersed in quiet reflective prayer rather than working at a computer, doing laundry, cleaning, cooking, and providing for others. I know how hard it can be to take time out to reflect and pray. I quickly came to realize, however, that consistent prayer is not something to put off until life slows down.

I was especially guilty of neglecting regular prayer while my first three children were young, often waiting for a quiet time to be with the Lord instead of allowing my prayer to take place in union with my daily duties. I wasted time feeling frustrated with my vocation since I thought it was preventing me from growing in holiness rather than providing an opportunity to seek out new graces to love and serve.

Now I try to unite my vocation as a wife and mother with prayer that sustains my daily activities and provides me with new graces. Each day I endeavor to remember that my goal is the same as that of the saints—to know, love, and serve Christ in the hope of being with him in heaven for all of eternity. Every moment that I am willing to both live fully and pray fully, the two united become an offering to God.

About This Book

Michele and I invite you to become a woman of prayer—to live your life prayerfully in the presence of God, who encourages all of us to take the next step in our relationship with him.

In the pages ahead, we will share the wisdom of the Church, lessons from the saints, stories of personal prayer (even miracles), and practical tips on integrating prayer into your daily life. Best of all, you will have an opportunity to try your hand at writing your own prayers, to express the things that are most pressing upon your heart.

Have you tried prayer journaling?

Each chapter is designed to help you go deeper into your prayer life. As you read along and spend time nurturing your relationship with God, we have made space for you to record your thoughts as a kind of ongoing conversation with God.

We hope this book will introduce you (if you are not already familiar with it) to the spiritual practice of prayer journaling, writing down your conversations with God as a natural part of your prayer life. You can use this book or purchase a separate journal to keep your prayer intentions and thoughts, notes from your spiritual reading, and things that strike you during prayer or scripture reading—you know, inspirations you feel from the Lord. A priest shared with me that sometimes when journaling, we write things we don't even know we are thinking! And so many times we have been blessed as we look back through the notes in our journal to glimpse God's handiwork in hindsight.

In the pages ahead, we've also included meditations we've written to help you focus your prayer, as well as prayer prompts for you to write your own prayers to God. At the end of this book you will find space to write your own spontaneous prayers and to record your intentions and the answers you receive. And we've also included a study guide. We encourage you to read this book with your friends in small–group study or to use the questions for personal reflection.

Pope Francis reminds us that prayer is "opening the door to the Lord, so that he can do something."[3] As we begin this journey together, may we open our hearts to God so he can radically transform us and fill our hearts with the gift of himself.

CHAPTER 1

The Power of Prayer
A Holy Invitation

Michele

And we have this confidence in him, that if we ask anything according to his will, he hears us. And if we know that he hears us in regard to whatever we ask, we know that what we have asked him for is ours.

—1 John 5:14–15

One hot summer day Emily and I sat in a small diner in Galena, Ohio, with our friend Angel. A sign on the wall read, "Life Is a Journey Filled with Unexpected Miracles." We believed the truth of this statement, as we were sitting with a real-life miracle. "I used to come here all the time when I was going through chemo and radiation," Angel said. "The waffles just melt in your mouth. It was the only thing I could eat sometimes."

A red Holy Spirit medallion hung from Angel's necklace, and its glimmer in the sunlight caught my eye. It was hard to believe we were with our friend; eighteen months had passed

since her doctor warned her that she had "maybe a year" to
live.

Angel's cancer journey was an amazing testament to the
power of prayer. A cradle Catholic, Angel was the youngest of
seven and had put herself through law school. She says that
her career as an attorney soon began to define who she was as
a person, and although she was well loved by her clients, her
work atmosphere was toxic and stressful. She was a devout
Catholic, and her faith was very important to her. Yet in recent
years she had experienced a great deepening of her faith and
prayer life. She had sensed God's call to draw closer to him,
so she began to seek him out.

In December 2016, Angel attended a retreat. She remembers going alone and feeling unworthy to be there. However,
she met a priest who prayed over her. During this special time
of intercessory prayer, she initially felt a tightening in her
throat. It was a feeling she had experienced many times under
stress. She began to cough incessantly and was barely able to
breathe. Then, suddenly, she felt a rush of oxygen. "It was like
electricity running up and down my body," she remembers, a
feeling of total peace. She knew she had encountered God at
that moment.

On the way home from the event, she started feeling a
lump in her throat that continued to get worse. On Christ-
mas Eve, she noticed swallowing became more difficult. As a
precaution her husband encouraged her to see a doctor, who
ordered an endoscopy (a noninvasive procedure that allows
the doctor to view your digestive tract with a camera). Angel
and her husband knew from the look on the doctor's face after
the procedure was over that the findings had not been good.
A tumor had been found and a biopsy was taken to be sent for
further examination.

It was a cold February day when she and her husband sat
down with the doctor to discuss the results of the biopsy, which
showed that she had stage three esophageal cancer. The doctor

told her that if she started chemotherapy immediately, she had "maybe a year to live." If she survived the complicated surgery, he said, she had about a 5 percent chance of living two years. In shock, Angel made her way out of the doctor's office and stood in the parking lot feeling sick. At just that moment, her phone rang. It was the local Catholic radio station, St. Gabriel Radio, asking if she would participate the following Tuesday in the *From the Chair* program, a call-in show featuring the bishop. The topic that day was going to be, "Time is a gift. What are we to do with that time?"

She agreed to call in and put away her phone. Turning to her husband, she said, "God will have a message for me Tuesday at 5:30 p.m."

At the appointed time she called in to speak to Bishop Campbell. "I was recently diagnosed with esophageal cancer," she told him. "All cancer is bad, but this cancer is going to silence me. My time will be spent in pain and silence, not being able to speak. What do I do with this time, how do I offer up this pain?"

As she had anticipated, God had a message for her that day, speaking through Bishop Campbell to remind her that we are not to deny the suffering that we face but embrace it. "There will be times that we are tempted to want to curse—why me, why now?" he told Angel. "We can't change it. But we can change our attitude toward it. How are we to face it? We face it with one of the great virtues: *Courage*."

He reminded Angel not to look too far in the future. "The time we possess is the time right here, right now. How do we use that time? It's up to us. Are we going to be paralyzed by fear, or do we use this time for good?

"The Lord gives us the ability to deal with the distress we have through the hands of medical personnel and through the comfort of our family and friends," the bishop continued. "We are not alone. Day by day, in each moment that we are given, pray that God encourage a stronger sense of his presence. Do not be afraid of weakness. Rather, depend on the gift of others. Ask God for clarity and understanding, a sense of peace and the gift of acceptance." He also encouraged Angel to seek the intercession of St. John Henry Newman that she would be healed.[1]

Angel took the bishop's words to heart and continued to pray. She was joined by numerous other friends who interceded on her behalf. Although the prognosis was grim, we all had hope for her physical and spiritual healing.

Hearing God's Voice in the Darkness

"How did your prayer life change after your diagnosis?" I asked Angel.

She smiled. "Michele, there is mechanical praying and then there is *praying*—when you speak to God and hear him. Hearing God's voice is imperative in growing in your prayer life. For me, the best way to hear God's voice is in eucharistic adoration." Angel has a designated time to go to adoration, every Thursday at 4:00 a.m. "It was in this place and time that I could hear God's voice the clearest."

Angel told me about a powerful time in prayer she experienced soon after her diagnosis. After beginning her hour with God with her usual prayer intention list, including all her friends and family, she heard in her heart, "Angel, you are going to be okay."

At first, she believed that the thought came from her own head, but then she heard it again. Like any attorney, she immediately put God in deposition mode. "God," she said, "I know what my okay is, but what is *your* okay?"

She laughed a little as she remembered that moment. Then she said to me, "You know, Michele, in that moment I knew, no matter what happened, if I lived or died, I was going to be okay. I had full acceptance of his will."

Angel began chemotherapy and radiation treatments to prepare her for surgery, which would involve relocating a major artery at the bottom of her stomach, removing most of her esophagus and part of her stomach, and moving her stomach up to the middle of her chest. The survival rate of this type of surgery was 50 percent. Amazingly, the operation was completed in two and a half hours, half the expected time. Even more surprising, the doctors said her organs and tissues were healthy, normal flesh, not damaged by radiation and chemo, as was expected. However, a short time later there was more bad news. In May 2018, a scan showed that the cancer had metastasized to the lungs. It was stage four esophageal cancer. She had just weeks to live.

Although the news was awful, Angel did not give up. "I know that God is with me—even in deepest despair and darkest moments. So often in the past I would look at my circumstances and feel hopeless. But the cancer was a kind of wake-up call, especially at work. I realized I needed to turn my anger at my coworkers and others to love, even when they were being jerks. I began to see my boss as a child of God, and I wanted to hug him instead of being angry with him. I wanted him to know how much he is loved by God."

As the anger faded from Angel's life, so did the cancer. At her next visit, the tumors in her lungs had shrunk 50 percent. In March 2019, just two years after the initial diagnosis, the CT scan showed the tumors were gone! Her doctor, a specialist in esophageal cancer, was shocked at the most recent scan report and told Angel he read it over multiple times, comparing it to the scan just three months prior, where the tumors were still present in her lungs. He had known only one other patient who survived two years with metastasized esophageal cancer.

Angel shared, "It is my belief that the reason I have been healed is because of all the intercessory prayers from my friends, family, and community. They are always with me, they don't fade away." She said, "I feel them more when I am in adoration. I can feel the prayers, like the breath of the Holy Spirit, the breath of prayers." She believes that because of all these prayers, she was granted more time, more strength, more understanding, and was able to hear the voice of God and accept his will.

"I would be in despair without prayer," Angel went on. "My greatest desire now is to help people understand the importance of their relationship with God in a deep prayer life, and I don't want them to have to get cancer to learn this lesson. Now, I try to connect with people who have cancer to pray with them and pray for them. I want to help them, to teach them to pray and listen to God. I have been given great graces and I want to share these graces with them.

"I know I will have a shorter life because of this cancer," Angel acknowledged. "But I believe in the power of prayer, and I have been given the gift of time, the best gift God can give me."

Partnering with God in Prayer

Angel's touching story reminds us of God's ability to work through even the darkest moments of our lives in order to draw us closer to him and to motivate us to live with eternity in mind. When we are troubled—or when someone we care about is in need of prayer—it is easy to turn to God. And yet, God urgently wants us to come to him daily—not just when we are in need. He wants us to experience his friendship in prayer, so that when the troubles come, we can trust him to do what is best for us. In that way we become true partners in prayer.

How do we begin to cultivate this kind of relationship with God?

Fr. Larry Richards writes, "As with all other friendships in our lives, our friendship with Jesus takes time and commitment. It is a give and take and not just one-sided. The only way to have a true friend is to spend time with them. We do this with Jesus when we pray. Do you have committed daily time with Jesus as your divine friend? He longs for you to be with him, and he calls you to this intimacy. And as with all friendship, we need to spend time with him each day."[2]

This is what God taught our friend Angel, as she made her way through those dark moments following her diagnosis. Can you think of a dark time in your own life, when God was trying to help you draw close to him in a similar way?

Is there a part of Angel's story that resonates with you? When was the last time God had your full attention? Write about it in the journaling space at the back of this book, or in your prayer journal.

Do You Have Time for God?

As busy women, we don't always make time with God a priority. There can be many reasons for this. For some, there are too many things pressing for time. For others, we don't know exactly what to say to God once we are alone with him. Sure, we find it easy to go to him when we need something, but he stands ready to offer us something even better: a true friendship with him. The *Catechism of the Catholic Church* states, "Yet the living and true God tirelessly calls each person to that mysterious encounter known as prayer. In prayer, the faithful God's initiative of love always comes first; our own first step is always a response" (2567).

Do you know God is calling you? That he loves you and is paying attention to you? God wants to spend time with you. God is always drawing you closer and asking that you come closer to him. He wants a dialogue with you, not just a monologue where you do all the talking. Prayer is that invitation from God to you; he initiates the conversation and is waiting for your reply. Prayer involves more than just talking, though; it involves the heart.

As I pondered these thoughts on prayer, I read this beautiful meditation by Fr. John Bartunek, who writes as though Jesus is speaking to us:

> Prayer is much simpler than you think. I am always with you, always at your side, and in your heart. I am always paying attention to you, thinking of you. I am always interested in what you are going through and what is in your mind and heart. Remember this, believe it, and prayer will become as natural as breathing. You never have to be alone. I am the one who knows you wholly and loves you no matter what. Live in the awareness of my presence; let me be your life's companion.[3]

Do you believe that?

Sometimes Catholics get a bad rap where prayer is concerned. I can remember working as a nurse at a crisis pregnancy center. Although it was founded by a devout Catholic, the volunteers were of many Christian faiths. One day two volunteers, not knowing I was Catholic, were chatting about a meeting they attended the previous evening. One woman spouted, "Then the funniest thing happened—they asked Bob to lead the prayer! You know Bob, he's *Catholic*, and well you know, those Catholics, they don't pray!"

I was shocked. *Of course Catholics pray!* I wanted to tell her. But I was young, and too shy to speak up—I couldn't even think of the words to respond. However, I knew that her impression couldn't be further from the truth. We pray all the time as Catholics, though we are often most comfortable with the rote prayers we learned as children. Yet God is calling us to so much more—he wants us to speak to him freely, from the heart.

Did you know that God wants to know your deepest desires? He wants to listen to your heartfelt cry and hear your honest response to what he asks of you. Of course, prayer can sometimes feel like a duty more than a friendship. There have been times when my prayer life has consisted only of going to Sunday Mass, where I would check in with the holy water and the Sign of the Cross and find myself checking out with the bulletin without actually talking to God! It was like going to a party and not saying hello to the host.

Have you ever felt like that? If so, maybe you'd like to explore with me just a bit, so that you can start moving toward a better, more personal relationship with God.

Let's Pray: Rest in Jesus' Presence

So where do we begin? A couple of years ago, I attended Mass at the Dublin Irish Fest, where Bishop Alphonsus Cullinan of Ireland talked on prayer:

> Where do we start? Just by talking to Jesus. Pour out your heart to him. Tell him everything—about your day, your family, your hopes, and your dreams. The more that you pray, the more that you will become attuned to the voice of God in your life. The more you talk to him and then *listen*, the more you will hear him. In moments of prayer, you may feel a calmness or a word of wisdom—that is Jesus. When you are at work and you feel that peace, that is Jesus. When you go to confession and feel that wave of mercy, that is Jesus. When you receive the Holy Eucharist and feel that presence, that is Jesus.[4]

Let's try it now, okay? Find a comfortable, quiet place (even if it's just a few minutes in the bathroom) to begin this divine dialogue. What is weighing on your mind and heart that you want the Lord to know about?

Don't be afraid to be honest. He knows it all anyway . . . but he wants to give you relief. He wants to lighten your burden. He wants to share your joy. So go ahead . . .

Tell Jesus what is on your mind. Or if you prefer, jot down a few things in the space at the back of this book, or in your prayer journal.

Okay, now that you've had a chance to let it all out, it's time for the second part: It's time to listen. Set down this book, close your eyes, take a deep breath . . . and as you let it out, invite Jesus to speak to you. Don't worry if nothing seems to happen. Just rest in his presence, and trust that he is at work in your heart even if you don't hear a word. Thank him for being with you, and ask him to continue to speak to you throughout the day. He does that in many ways—through other people, through circumstances, and especially through the scriptures.

Is this the first time you've ever thought about having a conversation with God?

Have you ever heard God speak to you? Write a bit about it in your journal.

Meet Your Heavenly Friend:
St. Gemma Galgani

God the Father, Jesus Christ, his mother Mary, and the angels are always present, although we cannot see them. The saints and angels are always praying for us and cheering us from the stands of heaven, which we read about in Hebrews 12: "Therefore, since we are surrounded by so great a cloud of witnesses, let us rid ourselves of every burden and sin that clings to us and persevere in running the race that lies before us while keeping our eyes fixed on Jesus, the leader and perfecter of faith" (Heb 12:1–2).

The saints serve a special dual purpose in the life of the believer—not only do they pray for us with great understanding but they also provide useful examples for us to follow.

Throughout this book we have included stories of some of our favorite saints. Right now, I'd like to tell you about one of mine! St. Gemma Galgani was born on March 12, 1878, in a small village near Lucca, Italy. Her mother was hesitant to call her Gemma since there was no saint with this name, yet the priest encouraged her, as there were many gems in heaven, and they hoped Gemma would someday join them.

Gemma's mother died when her daughter was only eight, and Gemma was sent to be raised by the Sisters of St. Zita. She was said to have a very "sanguine temperament and her blood was easily fired."[5] And yet despite her faults, Gemma had a great desire to become a saint. According to her biography, Gemma grew to prefer informal prayer, just talking with God throughout her day, instead of reciting formal prayers. She learned that by talking to God through all hours of the day and night, she was always in the presence of God.

Gemma was humble and keenly aware of her sins and imperfections, and wrote in a letter, "Gemma alone can do nothing. But together Gemma and Jesus can do all things!"[6]

Gemma grew into a beautiful young woman, yet she wanted only Christ as her spouse. When she was sixteen, she began to experience severe pain in her back. She had violent headaches, became deaf, lost all of her hair, and became paralyzed. She was diagnosed with tuberculosis of the spine, which was extremely difficult to treat and cure at the time. Treatment brought little relief, and Gemma was in excruciating pain, yet she accepted her cross and used this time of suffering to draw closer to Jesus and abandon her will to the will of God. When things looked hopeless, a priest recommended praying a novena to St. Margaret Mary Alacoque. At the end of the nine days, Gemma was miraculously and completely cured.

After her healing, Gemma progressed more deeply in prayer, especially by meditating on the Passion of Christ. Although she was denied entrance to the convent by the archbishop, she became a great mystic and received the stigmata (the wounds of Christ). In 1903 she contracted tuberculosis and died on April 11 of that year, on Holy Saturday. She was only twenty-five years old. St. Gemma was canonized in 1940.

St. Gemma's story reminds us that the path to sanctity often involves following in the footsteps of the saints and asking for their intercession. Which saints do you most admire and why? What have you learned from their lives, writings, and prayers? Write down your thoughts in your journal.

Deepen Your Prayer Life: Advice from St. Gemma

Take time out of your day to spend time with Jesus.

"Let us go to Jesus. He is all alone and hardly anyone thinks of Him. Poor Jesus!"[7]

When you cannot sleep, use that time to talk to Jesus.

"See, oh Jesus, even at night, those hours, those hours! I sleep, but Jesus my heart does not sleep. It watches with Thee at all hours."

When you first wake up in the morning, talk to Jesus. Take time to be near to his heart.

"Can You see that as soon as the day breaks I think of You? I am near You at every moment. . . . I love You, Jesus."

Pray before the Blessed Sacrament and receive Jesus in Holy Communion often.

"Oh, what immense joy and happiness my heart feels before Jesus in the Blessed Sacrament! . . . Jesus, soul of my soul, my

Paradise, holy Victim . . . behold, I am all Yours! I felt that You were seeking me and I ran to You!"

Ask Jesus for forgiveness even in little things (go to him in Confession for serious sins), and ask him to help you walk in his ways.

"My crucified God, behold me at Your feet. Do not reject me, a poor sinner, as I appear before You. I have offended You much in the past, my Jesus, but in the future I resolve to sin no more. My God, I put all my sins before You. I have considered them and realize they do not deserve Your pardon. But I beg of you to cast one glance upon Your sufferings and see how great is the worth of that Precious Blood that flows from your veins. My God, at this hour close Your eyes to my want of merit and open them to Your infinite merits. Since You, dear Jesus, have been pleased to die for my sins, grant me forgiveness for them all, that I may no longer feel their heavy burden, which presses me to the earth. My Jesus, help me, for I desire to become good, no matter what it may cost. Take away, destroy, root out completely all that You find in me that may be contrary to Your holy Will. At the same time I beg You, O Jesus, to enlighten me, that I may be able to walk in Your holy light. Amen."[8]

Prayer Prompt: Talk to Jesus

Take a few deep breaths, in through your nose and out through your mouth. Place yourself in the presence of God. Think of Jesus as he appears in one of your favorite stories in the gospels:

- Instead of busying yourself like Martha, imagine sitting beside Christ as Mary did (Lk 10:38–42). "Mary has chosen the better part."

- See Christ look into your eyes as he did the Samaritan woman at the well (Jn 4:4–26). "Whoever drinks the water I shall give will never thirst."
- Imagine his gaze of compassion as he passes by the weeping women of Jerusalem while carrying his Cross to Calvary (Lk 23:26–32). "Do not weep for me; weep instead for yourselves and for your children."

Now tell Jesus what is on your heart—your hopes, your fears, what you experienced today. Thank him for all the things for which you are most grateful. Then sit in silence and let Jesus speak to your heart. Ask him to reveal his will for your life. What did you hear? What would you most like to receive from him today? Write down your impressions and thoughts.

Read the opening scripture quote again: "And we have this confidence in him, that if we ask anything according to his will, he hears us. And if we know that he hears us in regard to whatever we ask, we know that what we have asked him for is ours" (1 Jn 5:14–15).

What is it that you would most like to ask from God today? Journal your petitions here or at the back of this book.

Close with a short prayer. Thank Jesus for this time you spent together. Ask him to help you grow closer to him each day.

The Basics of Prayer
Seek Him, Ask Him, Discover Him

Emily

Ask and it will be given to you; seek and you will find;
knock and the door will be opened to you. For everyone
who asks, receives; and the one who seeks, finds; and to
the one who knocks, the door will be opened.
—Matthew 7:7–8

In my younger years, my prayers would follow a similar pat-
tern. I'd start out, "Help me, Lord . . ." or "Lord, please bless
us with . . ." That would be followed by a few Hail Marys and
an Our Father. I would start my day with a bit of a survivor
mentality. I would give the Lord a list of the things my family
or I needed or wanted, and often these items would appear . . .
through the kindness of others who were totally unaware of my
prayer intentions.

15

These prayers were not rooted in a thriving prayer life, but rather were my attempt at simply enduring my day. I felt like I was on a sinking ship and desperately trying to barter with God, crying out, "Toss me a life raft, Lord, and I promise to do your will!"

So if these daily petitions weren't grounded in a deeper, more regular prayer habit, why did God answer them? I believe it wasn't mere coincidence; these answers were love notes from God seeking to get my attention and build trust. While this was rewarding in many ways, I came to realize that my dependence on "life raft prayers" was preventing me from experiencing something deeper and more satisfying.

Life began to change when I was willing to sit with the Lord and discover him through prayer and reading the scriptures on a regular basis. Making the time to digest his words and take them into my heart gave me a thirst for a deeper relationship with God and the courage to ask him for help, seek his will, and discover the life he was offering me. I found freedom through knowing I was loved and that I would be cared for. Slowly I came to realize that God didn't just want to provide the things my family needed; he also desired for me to trust him and see the larger picture. For example, when I was focused on figuring out how to get a baseball mitt for my son, he wanted my heart. Looking back, I can see that this process of seeking, discovering, and asking has revealed dreams and talents that had previously been suppressed because I was limiting God. God was not holding me back—I was the block to God's will by not fostering our relationship. I was limiting his will in my life by not discovering him in prayer.

"Adulting" in Prayer

There's a verse in the "love chapter" in 1 Corinthians 13 that says, "When I was a child, I used to talk as a child, think as a child, reason as a child; when I became a man, I put aside childish things" (v. 11). Of course, this is as true for women as it is for men. If we want a deep and loving relationship with another person, we have to be willing to put aside childish demands and invest ourselves in the other person.

The thing is, the same is true with God. For a long time, I ran after him with my childish demands to give me this or fix that. And yet, there came a time when I looked at my life and realized that many of the things I was asking God to "fix" would not have needed fixing if I'd only made better choices in the first place. The friendship that needed mending, for example, had been damaged by my own unwillingness to be vulnerable and allow others into the messiness of my life as I learned how to navigate being a young mother with a house full of children. I wouldn't ask for help when I felt like I was drowning and got used to the feeling that I was sinking all the time instead of learning how to thrive by accepting assistance from others. I felt unworthy of help and was embarrassed to admit I didn't have it all figured out, which left me in a place where I was becoming bitter and resentful toward my life. Pride was holding me back from not only seeking help but also navigating this challenging time in my life.

I realized that I needed to quit tossing up the life raft prayers and instead invite God to steer the ship, so to speak. Rather than start my day by asking God to throw me a life raft and rescue me, I needed to sit long enough to listen to what he was saying to me, most often through the scriptures or through encounters with other people.

And so, I began to approach God in a more deliberate, thoughtful way—investing in our friendship just as I do the other important relationships in my life. I began to *seek him* and connect with him in an intentional way at the start of each day. I began to *ask him* not just for what I needed, but also to show me what he wanted from me as well. And in the process, I began to *discover him*, his love and goodness, in a fresh, new way. As I continued to do these things, the childish relationship

I once had with God flourished into something better, richer, and deeper.

Instead of asking God to fix my messes, I gave him opportunities to tell me how to not get in trouble in the first place. It's not that bringing your intentions to the Lord and asking for his help is wrong—certainly it isn't. But I wanted to grow closer to him so I would know his will for me up front.

The "help me" prayer can be a legitimate way to start a conversation with our Lord and share our needs with him. Yet if this is the *only* way we pray, we risk missing out on so much the Lord wants to offer us! The truth is that what we put into prayer is what we typically get out. This is true with anything—dieting, working out, improving at a sport or hobby—they all require an investment of our time and energy in order to realize gains.

I have come to appreciate that when we take time to develop an active and personal prayer life, we can better navigate our lives and see God's will play out in both the good and not-so-good times. Jesus wants us to bring to him our daily needs, and yet he offers us so much more. I oftentimes feel like the woman who met Jesus at the well in the book of John, asking Jesus for water for my thirst, yet Jesus wants to give us living water!

He tells the woman, "Everyone who drinks this water will be thirsty again; but whoever drinks the water I shall give will never thirst; the water I shall give will become in him a spring of water welling up to eternal life" (Jn 4:13–14). Jesus is inviting us to forge a relationship with him through an active prayer life, which is always drawing us closer to him and will last into eternity. Yet we must answer Jesus' invitation. "Prayer is the soul's response to God's initiative."[1]

How would you describe your relationship with God? How do you seek, ask, and discover God? How has your relationship with God changed over time? Write about it in your prayer journal, or in the space at the back of this book.

Love Notes from God

If we ask God to help us grow closer to him, he will certainly grant us this desire. The greatest example in my own life of a "love note" from God happened recently when my brother, a Catholic priest, bought a ticket at a charity auction and won the grand prize: an all-inclusive trip to visit and pray in the footsteps of Jesus in Bethlehem, Galilee, Nazareth, and Jerusalem. My two siblings were unable to accept the gift since they both had young babies at home, my dad's health wasn't good at the time, and my brother was already heading to the Holy Land on pilgrimage the following month, so we were offered the trip. Ten days in the Holy Land, kid-free!

My husband and I had been to the Holy Land very early in our marriage, and now, twenty years later, we received the same invitation to walk in Jesus' footsteps and renew our love for him through this pilgrimage. I felt completely unworthy of the gift, and yet my husband and I knew it was an invitation to a deeper relationship and an incredible opportunity to renew our prayer life, so we gratefully accepted. This was not the answer to a specific prayer petition, but it was an answer in a very real way to a silent yearning in my heart for a recharge to my faith as we worked through all the challenges of raising a large Catholic family in the modern world.

When was the last time you received a "love note" from God? Likely it wasn't a free trip to the Holy Land—but it was a meaningful reminder of God's providence in your life. Write about it in your journal.

Perhaps the most impactful part of our trip was taking a boat ride on the Sea of Galilee. We boarded early in the morning as the sun was just rising and were blessed with calm seas. Our guide explained how the topography of the surrounding hillsides could cause very strong winds to occur quickly, resulting in rough seas. As I enjoyed the peace and quiet and the significance of this place where so much of Jesus' teaching ministry took place, the story of Jesus appearing to the disciples during a storm in the dark of night came to mind. We read in the Gospel of Matthew,

> During the fourth watch of the night, he came toward them, walking on the sea. When the disciples saw him walking on the sea they were terrified. "It is a ghost," they said, and they cried out in fear. At once [Jesus] spoke to them, "Take courage, it is I; do not be afraid." Peter said to him in reply, "Lord, if it is you, command me to come to you on the water." He said, "Come." Peter got out of the boat and began to walk on the water toward Jesus. But when he saw how [strong] the wind was he became frightened; and, beginning to sink, he cried out, "Lord, save me!" Immediately Jesus stretched out his hand and caught him, and said to him, "O you of little faith, why did you doubt?" After they got into the boat, the wind died down. Those who were in the boat did him homage, saying, "Truly, you are the Son of God." (14:25–33)

What is Jesus saying to you in this Gospel reading (Mt 14:25–33)? Can you hear him calling you much like he called Peter? Write down your thoughts in your prayer journal.

As I pondered this scripture, I came to see it as a metaphor for the Christian life and an invitation to take my relationship with Christ to a new level. In that moment, I felt Jesus calling me to stop clinging to my boat being tossed about on the waves, to step out onto the water and move toward him. I was reminded to keep my gaze fixed on him so as not to look at the crashing waves around me and lose faith, to trust in him fully lest I begin to sink. I imagined how tightly Peter must have clung to our Lord after being pulled out of the water and how safe he must have felt in Jesus' embrace. It occurred to me that this is what true prayer must be like. I can't even begin to express the peace I felt in that moment.

How many times in our own life does Jesus call us to have courage and to place our eyes on him and have faith? Do we truly believe that nothing is impossible for God, that he is always trying to help us, sending us love notes, answering our prayers, and calling us into a deep and lasting relationship with him? Jesus offers to calm our storms in life and provide us stability and direction. He stands ready to answer our cries for help through our petitions and prayers, and he is calling us to step out in faith to him. Let us pray for courage to face our troubles and bring our intentions to the Lord.

What storms are raging in your life? Are you willing to step out of the boat and place your eyes on Christ? Jot down your thoughts in your prayer journal.

Build a Prayer Plan

Prayer is a compass that directs us on our journey, our daily ration that imparts strength. Without prayer, our faith drifts away and we lose our bearings. Prayer is essential to gain a new perspective on our lives and experience the promptings of the Holy Spirit. Without prayer, we lack the grace to grow from our life moments, whether good or bad. Prayer is not just for busy people but for those who are young, youthful, suffering, waiting, wondering, hurting, needing, and resting in their final years of life. Prayer is for everyone.

Prayer is not a promise of smooth sailing but a way to manage the inevitable storms of life. Prayer is a stabilizer that teaches us how to remain Christ focused in a world that is completely unfocused and full of distractions. Prayer gives us the direction we need to have "sea legs" in the midst of our daily trials and difficulties. Faith is a gift that allows us to see the hand of the Lord throughout our day. When uttered in faith, our prayers do not just consist of what we need ("Give us this day our daily bread") but offer praise and thanksgiving for all we have and express our greatest desire, to unite our will to that of God the Father. This entrustment is right in the good times and bad, the bitter and sweet moments.

St. Augustine once said, "My desire was not to be more certain of you but to be more stable in you."[2] When we seek to do the will of God and develop a relationship with Christ through prayer, we become stable and confident in our actions and grow into the people we are called to be. God is present in us at all times. When we allow God to work in our life, we begin to see the more significant connections and recognize God calling us to a closer relationship with him. The goal of our prayer life is to be more stable in Christ, which will bear tremendous fruits in our soul and for those around us.

One of the most important ways to become stable and confident of God's constant presence in our lives is to develop a personal prayer plan—a daily appointment with God that is reserved for him alone. It may take some creativity and persistence, but as you make God a priority, taking time to *seek, ask,* and *discover,* you will find renewed energy and strength to face the challenges of your day.

What is your prayer plan? When and where can you spend daily time with God, just the two of you? How can you make that a priority? Write down your plan in your prayer journal or the back of this book.

Here are some important things I've discovered as I've developed my own prayer plan.

Prayer is a peaceful oasis that helps us rise above chaos.

St. Margaret Mary once said, "He is more precious than all His gifts. However, of these gifts, that of His pure love surpasses all the others."[3] Seeking Christ can be a difficult challenge, especially when you are surrounded by the chaotic busyness of life. With all the noise, it can be hard to concentrate on the spiritual life and dedicate the time needed to develop it. The Lord wants to offer us a deep and personal prayer life that will feed us and sustain us while focusing on our end game—heaven. Jesus knows us, and he gives us the graces to take baby steps in our faith life. It is our job to be open to him and pray. The love of Christ is the greatest gift we can ever receive.

As a busy, working wife and mom with seven children, I know it can be easy to put prayer on the back burner and subscribe to the popular idea that by just living my life the best way I can and offering it to God I am "praying always." Indeed, I do honor God by this type of intentional way of living, but if I'm honest with myself, I also recognize that with that mentality I actually end up praying very little.

Praying at a specific time helps to cultivate healthy prayer habits. It is with our whole being that we pray, or else it is useless; it is from within the heart that these prayers come forth since this is where God resides within us. Our heart is where the prayer is formed and released, whether we are praying memorized prayers or engaging in a spontaneous outpouring of the heart. The heart is always involved in prayer.[4]

A daily habit of prayer helps us to see all the ways God blesses us.

Without prayer, we miss out on what God is offering us every day! I know that even if I rise and spend time with the Lord in prayer, I will continue to experience significant challenges and difficulties, but prayer gives me the grace to invite Christ

into those moments and allows me to accept them and work
through them. We learn in scripture, "Cast all your worries
upon him because he cares for you" (1 Pt 5:7).

My life is full of worries and stress, so prayer is essential
every day. Prayer has become my fuel, my daily strength and
reminder that at any moment I can call upon the Lord. I know
I am not alone. Prayer is more than just a way to get what we
want; it helps us navigate through our lives and grow in holiness. Without prayer, darkness creeps into our soul, and we
begin to feel overwhelmed, confused, and uncertain. Without
prayer, our faith drifts away, and any quiet time we have is
filled with distractions that leave us feeling empty.

Consistent prayer leads us to deeper prayer, including meditation.

A consistent prayer habit enables us to cultivate not only *regular* encounters with God, but *deeper* ones as well. By showing
up for prayer each day, we give ourselves time to slow down
enough to meditate. The *Catechism* tells us that "meditation is
above all a quest," or a journey leading us to God. "The mind
seeks to understand the why and how of the Christian life,
in order to adhere and respond to what the Lord is asking"
(*CCC*, 2705).

For many of us, the thought of Christian meditation is
foreign. St. Francis de Sales shares that "if you contemplate
him frequently in meditation, your whole soul will be filled
with him, you will grow in his likeness, and your actions will
be molded on his."[5] Christian prayer is not the emptying of self,
as is the focus of many Eastern religions, but rather the filling of
the soul with the presence of God and learning to communicate
with the Father. Through meditation we seek to enter into a
love relationship with Christ. Meditation can be challenging.
But "even if our prayer doesn't seem to be bearing fruit on the
level of our conscious intellect, it may very well bear fruit on

the level of strengthening our will."[6] Don't get discouraged; rather, seek out Christ in this quiet and meaningful way. Without meditation, we cannot go deeper in our faith life.

Let's Pray: Lectio Divina

Each day we are invited to go deeper into our prayer life through the use of meditation. One of my favorite ways of meditating is to pray using sacred scripture through a practice known as lectio divina. *Lectio divina*, or "divine reading," is a way of reading scripture with the intention of being in communion with God and understanding the Word as it is spoken to our hearts.

I remember the first time I prayed with scripture, instead of reading it as I would a piece of literature. I spent time prayerfully focusing on the words of God and reflecting on their meaning in my life in the here and now. When you practice lectio divina, you invite Christ to speak to you. Let's try it together—and don't forget to take notes and write down your thoughts in your prayer journal or the back of this book:

Begin by preparing your heart.

Place yourself in God's presence and pray, "Dear Lord, thank you for giving us your Word. Help us to hear your voice and respond to your call. Amen."

Read a selected passage of scripture slowly.

Here is one sample, but you can select any scripture verse you would like to meditate on:

> Jesus said to his disciples: "Amen, amen, I say to you, whatever you ask the Father in my name he will give you. Until now you have not asked anything in my name; ask and you will receive, so that your joy may be complete." (Jn 16:23–24)

Spend a moment in silence.

What strikes you from this passage?

Reread the scripture slowly.

Then spend a moment in silence. What do you hear and see this time? How is God speaking to you?

Reread the scripture a third time.

Then spend a moment in silence. How is God inviting you to change? Write down what you feel God is calling you to do.

End by spending a moment thanking God.

Offer a simple prayer such as, "Dear Lord, thank you for this time spent with your Word. Thank you for speaking to my heart. Please help me change the things in my life that need to be changed and follow your will. Amen."

When we take time out to meditate, we allow Christ to lead us into a deeper relationship that will bear more fruit in our lives.

Meet Your Heavenly Friend: St. Teresa of Calcutta

Mother Teresa provides a powerful example of how prayer is spiritual fuel; daily prayer sustained her mission to love and serve the poorest of the poor. Her fervent practice of prayer stabilized her life and helped her answer the call to "get out of the boat" and serve others.

Mother Teresa of Calcutta was born Agnes Gonxha Bojaxhiu on August 26, 1910, in what is now the Republic of Macedonia, to an Albanian family; she later became a citizen of India. Her father died when she was eight years old, and her Catholic mother worked hard to run an embroidery business and provide for the family. In 1928, Agnes left home to join the Sisters of Loreto, an Irish order that was located in Calcutta, India. It is believed to be the last time she saw her mother and her sister.

Agnes received a new name, Sister Teresa, in honor of St. Thérèse of Lisieux, her patron saint. In 1937, she became Mother Teresa. While living in Calcutta during the 1930s and '40s, she taught at St. Mary's Bengali Medium School for the Sisters of Loreto. In 1946, while on a long train ride, she experienced "a call within a call" that resulted in her leaving the Loreto sisters to begin a new order, the Missionaries of Charity. According to Mother Teresa, "[We are] to quench the thirst of Jesus for souls, for love, for kindness, for compassion, for delicate love. By each action done to the sick and the dying, I quench the thirst of Jesus for love of that person."[7]

On October 7, 1950, the new congregation of the Missionaries of Charity was officially established as a religious institute for the Archdiocese of Calcutta, and quickly the order spread around the world. This pious and holy woman went on to become an international sensation. The rich, the poor, the powerful, the educated, and the faithful were all drawn to her warm smile, deep faith, and remarkable service to others. In 1979 she received the Nobel Peace Prize, and she was honored by governments, universities, and other organizations throughout the world. Despite the fame, she rejected the possibility of fortune and focused on her desire to serve Christ through the poor and rejected of society. When presented with awards and formal recognition, she would often say "for the glory of God and in the name of the poor."

Mother Teresa died from heart failure at eighty-seven years of age on September 5, 1997. Her funeral was truly an international celebration with world leaders and the poor alike gathered to honor this remarkable woman. At the time of her death, the Missionaries of Charity had grown to more than four thousand sisters who cared for not only the poor of Calcutta

but also the sick, dying, refugees, disabled, blind, and victims
of all types of natural disasters in 133 countries. The sisters
were, and are, a living example of her life motto, "Love in
action."[8] She was beatified by her friend, Pope John Paul II, in
2003 and was canonized in St. Peter's Square on September 4,
2016, by Pope Francis.

Just Keep Praying:
Advice from St. Teresa of Calcutta

Mother Teresa knew that her greatest source of strength and
consolation was prayer. She spent many, many hours in prayer,
especially in adoration. The Missionaries of Charity make it
their mission not only to spend hours a day in silent prayer but
also "to bring prayer into the lives of the poor by praying with
them and helping them personally to experience the power of
prayer. Besides encouraging personal and family prayer, we
also encourage meditation and prayerful readings of the Word
of God and the inspiring lives of holy people."[9]

Many books have been written by and about Mother
Teresa, and prayer was one of her favorite subjects. After her
death, it was discovered that she spent years in a "dark night
of the soul," unable to sense God's presence. She would say,
"The feeling of not being loved by God and the feeling that
God doesn't even exist are the best evangelizers, because they
truly understand the experience of a multitude of souls in this
world."[10] Despite being unable to sense the presence of God,
she continued to pray and to do what she believed she had
been called to do.

Have you ever tried talking to God and felt as though no
one was listening? It happens to all of us sometimes—even
Mother Teresa! And so, we can learn from her example to continue walking in faith, knowing that we can trust God is present even when we cannot feel he is there.

Here are some other important lessons on prayer that we can learn from Mother Teresa:

The important thing is to pray and pray and pray.

Mother Teresa would say, "The more you pray, the more you will love to pray—and the more you love to pray, the more you will pray!"[11] She believed that "we need prayer to understand God's love for us."[12]

If you cannot pray, give it to God.

Mother Teresa said, "When we have nothing to give—let us give Him that nothingness. When we cannot pray—let us give that inability to Him. . . . Let us ask Him to pray in us, for no one knows the Father better than He. No one can pray better than Jesus."[13]

Hear God in silence.

"God speaks in the silence of our hearts, and we listen. Then, out of the fullness of our heart, we speak and He listens. And that is prayer."[14]

Prayer is our fuel.

"Without blood there is no life in the body; without gas in the car—no driving. But also, without prayer the soul is dead."[15]

Mother Teresa teaches us that our true identity is not in our nationality or citizenship but rather in Christ Jesus. "By blood, I am Albanian. By citizenship, an Indian. By faith, I am a Catholic nun. As to my calling, I belong to the world. As to my heart, I belong entirely to the Heart of Jesus."[16]

Prayer Prompt: The Our Father

Take a moment and reflect on how much God loves you and desires a deep and personal relationship with you. He wants you to feel his love and know that he is offering you so much more than you can imagine!

Using the lectio divina practice introduced on page 25, let's pray the Our Father slowly, with our whole heart. Let's think of Jesus teaching this prayer to his disciples and how this prayer has been passed on from generation to generation. The Lord's Prayer "is truly the summary of the whole gospel" (*CCC*, 2761) and well worth praying.

As you begin, find a place of quiet. Think about your earliest experiences with the Our Father. Who taught it to you? To whom are you going to teach this prayer? Ask the Holy Spirit to speak to you through this prayer in a new way.

Let us pray:

> Our Father in heaven,
>   hallowed be your name,
>   your kingdom come,
>   your will be done,
>   on earth as in heaven.
>   Give us today our daily bread;
>   and forgive us our debts,
>   as we forgive our debtors;
>   and do not subject us to the final test,
>   but deliver us from the evil one.

If you forgive others their transgressions, your heavenly Father will forgive you. But if you do not forgive others, neither will your Father forgive your transgressions. (Mt 6:9–15)

Share with Jesus how you feel about the Our Father. What parts of the prayer do you struggle with? What phrases jump out at you and speak to your heart? Is there someone you need to forgive right now?

What struck you about praying the Our Father slowly and focusing on each word? Record your thoughts in your prayer journal.

Now take a moment and listen . . . truly open your heart and listen to what Jesus has to say to you. Can you hear him say, "I thirst"? This is the phrase he used on the Cross. He is thirsting for a relationship with us. He wants us to go deeper. How can this happen in your life?

CHAPTER 3

Living Pray-Fully
Praying through the Day

Michele

> Pray without ceasing.
>
> —1 Thessalonians 5:17

One of the most spiritually transforming moments in my life was a "do-it-yourself" retreat I made one weekend shortly after I graduated from college. It involved working my way slowly through a book by Fr. Michael E. Gaitley, *Consoling the Heart of Jesus*, based on the Spiritual Exercises of St. Ignatius of Loyola. I purchased this book because I knew the author in college and wanted to support his writing; I had no idea how much it was going to impact my prayer life.

As I read the book on retreat, I was immediately enraptured by the meditative writings, and I prayed the words on the page as if they were my own:

"Jesus, I thirst for you. Help me to thirst for you more."
"Use me, Jesus. Form me into a saint."

33

"Make up for all my faults. I trust in you."
"With Mary's help, I give you my help."[1]

As I pored over the pages, I had a spiritual awakening. This retreat changed the way I looked at prayer forever. I came to the stark realization that I was not growing in my prayer life. The busyness of part-time work, two children (at the time), and many volunteer roles left little time for serious prayer.

Although I realized the defect in my spiritual life, I didn't have a remedy to my problem. My life was only going to get busier and more demanding. I craved quiet time alone in prayer but struggled to make it happen. Yet I knew the scriptures instructed us to "pray without ceasing" (1 Thes 5:17), to continually seek the Lord throughout the day. I asked the Lord, "How can I make this happen in my life?"

One day the Lord spoke clearly to me as I sat in the car. I had been running some errands and had only twenty minutes until it was time to pick up my daughter from preschool. There was not enough time for an additional errand or to stop home, and my youngest was asleep in the car seat. I decided to pull into the school parking lot and listen to the local Catholic radio station and catch up on some email. *Women of Grace* with Johnnette Benkovic was on, and her words caught my attention. She was discussing the very same plight in her life, trying to find time to pray. She shared, "I heard God say to me, 'Johnnette, I'll give you the time to pray, you just have to use it.'"

It clicked in my head: "God is talking to me too!" I was sitting, parked in my car, in total silence. What a great fifteen minutes this could be if I spent it in prayer instead of wasting it on email. I asked God to show me the times during the day I was "wasting" and to help me use them as opportunities to pray. As I looked for more moments to pray during the day, more opportunities came available. I also became more purposeful in creating time during my day to spend time with God. It may not always be a long time, but even five or ten minutes in conversation with God has borne good fruit and helped me know his will for my life.

How do we begin integrating prayer into our daily life? First, ask God for his help! We can try this right now. Take a deep breath in through your nose and breathe out through your mouth. Place yourself in his presence.

Tell God how you are feeling. Express your desire to spend more time with him in prayer. Ask him to show you the moments in your day he wants you to pray and be with him. Ask him to allow you to see when you can spend time with him and give you the strength and perseverance to use that time and not waste it. Invite Jesus to speak to you. Don't worry if nothing seems to happen at first. Just rest in his presence, and trust that he is at work in your heart even if you don't hear a word. Thank him for being with you, and ask him to continue to speak to you throughout the day. He does that in many ways—through other people, through circumstances, and especially through the scriptures.

What's on your mind today? As you sit quietly in God's presence and scattered thoughts cross your mind, jot them down in your prayer journal—then set them mentally aside. Bring yourself gently back to sitting with Jesus. Don't let anything come between you.

Emily and I have been surprised at how God has opened up the time for us to spend with him during our busy days and also how God has called us to carve out time for prayer. Below are some of our favorite tips and practical advice for weaving prayer throughout your day.

Mornings matter.

Mornings are a valuable time to set ourselves up for spiritual success throughout the day. St. Francis de Sales suggests that when you pray, "let it be early in the morning, when your mind will be less cumbered, and fresh after the night's rest."[2] Morning is the best time for me to pray, and as I grow in my prayer life, I slowly increase this time each morning. It's an act of discipline to get up an extra fifteen or twenty minutes early, but I find it can be the best twenty minutes of my day!

The purpose of prayer is to know God's will for your life and to help conform your will to his will (not the other way around as we may think!). We read in the book of Romans, "Do not conform yourselves to this age but be transformed by the renewal of your mind, that you may discern what is the will of God, what is good and pleasing and perfect" (Rom 12:2).

If you are a beginner to prayer, consider starting each new day with just this one sentence: "Lord, show me what you want me to do today, and don't let my will get in the way of yours." When we make room for the Holy Spirit, we allow God to not only touch our hearts but also open our eyes to the needs of those we're called to love and serve throughout our day. This simple prayer helps us to begin seeing God's hand in our daily life.

Read the scriptures.

God speaks to us through his living Word, the holy scriptures. The Bible is the inspired Word of God—and he is still speaking to us from its pages! Reading and praying over the scriptures leads to growth in our spiritual life. As we ponder the words of scripture, we use our senses to see, hear, feel, and understand what those who have gone before us endured. Scripture is the greatest love story, one of a God who is constantly drawing us closer into relationship with him.

Reading scripture has become one of my priorities each morning. Fr. Larry Richards is famous for the saying, "No Bible, no breakfast; no Bible, no bed." I like to have my coffee and oatmeal first, because I can't focus when I'm hungry, but my motto is, "No Bible, no email" (or social media). Always read scripture first! One of the easiest ways to begin meditating on God's Word is to ponder the daily Mass readings. The readings for Mass are the same all over the world and chosen by day or theme. If you plan on going to Mass, this also serves as preparation. Since I'm so often distracted with kids during Mass and can't give my full attention to the liturgy, having already meditated on the scriptures is tremendously helpful.

Thanks to the internet, the readings of the day are always available to us. My favorite way to reflect on the daily readings is to use a direct email I receive from Fr. Burke Masters's blog. Each day he chooses one of the Mass readings (first reading or the gospel) and writes a meditation on its meaning. He always gives me so much to think about and ponder throughout my day.

If you are striving to go a little deeper in meditative practices with the gospels, I highly recommend The Better Part App. This app is a tool to help you "engage more actively in the quest of Christian meditation so you can reap more fruits of spiritual growth."[3] It is also available in book form if you prefer a hard copy. Each section contains a reading from the gospels and commentary based on four themes: Christ the Lord, Christ the Teacher, Christ the Friend, and Christ in My Life.

Another phenomenal (and transformative) program is *Pray40Days* by Fr. Michael Denk. This free website and app guides you through different types of prayer that will "immerse you in the life of Christ, fill you with the Holy Spirit, and allow you to be loved by the Father."[4] I especially enjoy using this program because the app has an audio component, so I put on my noise-cancelling headphones, close my eyes, and allow Fr. Denk to lead me through prayer. Both of these programs have helped me advance in my prayer life more than ever before.

Peg a prayer.

One of Emily's apostolates is a short segment she offers daily on Catholic Radio called "A Mother's Moment." (Don't let the title fool you; these spiritual gems are for everyone!) A

reflection she offered called "Peg a Prayer" is one of my favorites. This phrase was coined to help us to "peg" or associate a
daily activity with a prayer.

For example, tape a prayer card to your bathroom mirror
so that you can make a short morning offering when you're
brushing your teeth. When doing the laundry, pray for the
family member whose laundry you are handling. Another one
of our favorites is the "kitchen sink prayer." A friend of ours
gave us this beautiful idea. Instead of allowing resentment and
anger to build up while hard at work washing dishes at the
kitchen sink, she suggested I put a prayer card in my window
that I could read while doing the dishes. My sink prayer is
the "Prayer of Divine Transformation from Within" from the
Diary of St. Faustina: "I want to be completely transformed into
Your mercy and to be Your living Reflection, O Lord."[5] So as
I scrub my dishes clean, this grace-filled prayer helps me also
transform my soul!

Make your car a chapel.

Making your car a chapel also enables you to incorporate
prayer into your day. On average, Americans spend just under
an hour a day in the car.[6] Can you imagine what might happen
if we spent that hour talking to God instead of yelling at the
other drivers (or the kids in the back seat)?

My go-to prayer during quiet car time is the Rosary.
Although I can't close my eyes and meditate on the Mysteries,
I certainly can call to mind the life of Christ, and the rhythmic
prayers of the Hail Marys, Glory Bes, and Our Fathers give me
time to pause and reflect while placing myself in the presence
of God.

Another great way to pray in the car is with praise music!
I fill my playlist with music from Out of Darkness, His Own,
Audrey Assad, Matt Maher, Danielle Rose, Sarah Kroger,
Fr. Rob Galea, Sarah Hart, Emily Wilson, Amanda Vernon,
Ben Walther, Teresa Peterson, Tori Harris, Taylor Tripodi, PJ

Anderson, and other Catholic artists. As I drive, our family loves to belt out the words (even though some of us are not the greatest singers), and it always lifts my spirit and connects me to God. Music and singing can provide a deep, personal encounter with God, and I oftentimes find myself singing the words (praying) throughout the day, without even realizing it!

Pray with the Eucharist.

Before Christ died on the Cross for our sins, he gave us the Eucharist. The *Catechism* teaches us, "Since Christ was about to take his departure from his own in his visible form, he wanted to give us his sacramental presence; since he was about to offer himself on the cross to save us, he wanted us to have the memorial of the love with which he loved us 'to the end,' even to the giving of his life. In his Eucharistic presence he remains mysteriously in our midst as the one who loved us and gave himself up for us" (1380).

Going to Sunday Mass is the highlight of my week and an important part of my prayer life. Mass should transform us and give us a clearer vision of what we are to do that day (and week). I know I cannot accomplish all Christ is asking of me if I do not spend at least one hour a week with him in the eucharistic celebration. One of my favorite quotes is from St. John Paul II: "The Eucharist is the secret of my day. It gives strength and meaning to all my activities of service to the Church and to the whole world. . . . Let Jesus in the Blessed Sacrament speak to your hearts. It is he who is the true answer of life that you seek. He stays here with us: he is God with us. Seek him without tiring, welcome him without reserve, love him without interruption: today, tomorrow, forever."[7]

As a Catholic woman, I know I need the Eucharist to sustain me, and I try to attend Mass as frequently as possible. It helps me open my heart to what God wants me to do that day and gives me the strength to persevere. Fr. John Riccardo writes in his book *Heaven Starts Now*, "Obviously we need to go to Sunday Mass. But ask yourself this: is it possible for me to achieve greatness when I am feeding on the Eucharist only once a week? Once we've really come to understand, objectively speaking, that the Eucharist is the *greatest* source of strength that we could ever encounter in our lives, why wouldn't we want to go more often? Some of us can't go to Mass more than once a week because of work. But maybe we can try to get there once during the week, in addition to Sunday."[8]

If you are unable to attend daily Mass, eucharistic adoration is another powerful way to connect with God during the day. At any time you can stop and make a little visit with Jesus!

Praying in front of the Eucharist (eucharistic adoration) allows us to encounter Christ and hear his voice in our hearts. Jesus is truly present in the tabernacle and when exposed in the monstrance on the altar. John Paul II writes, "Jesus waits for us in this sacrament of love. Let us be generous with our time in going to meet Him in adoration and in contemplation that is full of faith and ready to make reparation for the great faults and crimes of the world. May our adoration never cease."[9]

Many parishes offer adoration at specific times during the week, and some have it twenty-four hours a day. Even if you only have fifteen minutes, stop in church and have a conversation with Jesus; he is waiting for you.

Let's Pray: What Is an Examen?

The daily Examen is a spiritual practice developed by St. Ignatius of Loyola that helps us look back over our day and see how God was at work in it. Each time we make an Examen, we give thanks to God, acknowledge our shortcomings, and plan for the new day.

Before my head hits the pillow, I take ten minutes with this simple formula for prayer. I like using the Examen prayer app by Fr. Michael Denk (see theprodigalfather.org), but you can use any written Examen guide to lead you through a reflection on your day. (We have included a sample Examen exercise in the "Prayer Prompt" section at the end of this chapter.)

As we find moments in our day to connect with God on a more intimate level, we grow in our prayer life and prayer becomes more of a habit. The *Catechism* reminds us, "We cannot pray 'at all times' if we do not pray at specific times, consciously willing it" (2697). I promise you, if you invest time in speaking to God and hearing his voice each day, your life will be transformed.

Meet Your Heavenly Friend: St. Gianna Beretta Molla

St. Gianna is a beautiful model of faith for all women. As a wife, mother, and physician, she embodied what it means to pray fully, staying close to God throughout each day.

Gianna Francesca Beretta was born on the feast of St. Francis of Assisi, October 4, 1922, in the Lombardy region of Italy. She was the twelfth child in her family; only seven lived to adulthood. Her family was devoutly Catholic, and she went to Mass every day with her mother. Although she was "not a brilliant student,"[10] her family encouraged her to study hard, and she eventually earned good grades. She had health concerns that caused her to miss some school, but Gianna used this time to play piano, paint, do housework, and become involved with Catholic Action, "a movement whose aim was to mobilize the Catholic laity to live a more intense spiritual life."[11]

Both of Gianna's parents died in 1942, but she continued with her studies and remained involved with Catholic Action, becoming president of the Young Women's Branch from 1946 to 1949. In 1949, Gianna received her medical certificate and opened her practice. She later took specialized courses in pediatrics and obstetrics. Although she wanted to work in the mission field, her health prevented her from doing so, so she worked diligently in her medical practice in Italy, treating it as her home mission work.

When she was thirty-two years old, Gianna met Pietro Molla and they quickly fell in love, marrying in September 1956 and settling in Ponte Nuovo, Italy. Gianna continued her medical practice and volunteer work with Catholic Action. She became president of the Women's Branch and held that position until she died.

Gianna and Pietro had three children between 1956 and 1959. They spent their time raising their family, working, traveling, and enjoying time together. In 1961 Gianna was expecting their fourth child after two miscarriages. The doctors discovered a noncancerous fibroid in her uterus and gave her the choice of an abortion (losing the baby), a hysterectomy (losing the baby and her uterus), or removal of the fibroma. Gianna chose the third option, with full knowledge that it was the most risky for her own life. She underwent surgery to remove the fibroma and was able to resume her medical practice during the final months of her pregnancy. As the child grew in her womb, Gianna prayed fervently for her family. She was still in danger, and although she hoped she would be spared, she insisted that if there were complications, the baby's life was to come first.

On April 21, 1962, Giovanna Emanuela was born via cesarean section. After the delivery, Gianna developed septic peritonitis and experienced severe pain. Knowing she was dying, she requested to be sent home from the hospital to be with her family. She died on April 28. Her daughter is still alive today and practices geriatric medicine. She travels the world telling the story of her mother's heroic sacrifice.

Gianna Beretta Molla was canonized by Pope John Paul II on May 16, 2004. In his homily he stated she was a "messenger of divine love."[12] St. Gianna is the first canonized woman physician and is a faithful intercessor for every "working mom."

One of my favorite books on St. Gianna is a compilation of the letters she wrote to her husband over the years. Many of the writings of the saints that I read are filled with holy thoughts, prayers, and visions, yet in these letters, St. Gianna reveals that she was like many of us in her ordinary life. She shares about her daily struggles and the juggling of her responsibilities as a physician, wife, and mother.

In her notes to Pietro, she communicates about the simple things of life we all encounter: grocery lists, broken washing machines, driving a car, and even what she watched on television! Yet her ordinary life filled with extraordinary love shows all women that sanctity is within our reach in this modern day if we live a life of prayer and sacrifice.

On the Spiritual Life: Advice from St. Gianna Beretta Molla

St. Gianna identified six important components of the spiritual life: morning and evening prayer (not in bed, but on your knees), attending Holy Mass and Holy Communion, meditating at least ten minutes each day, frequently visiting the Blessed Sacrament (eucharistic adoration), and praying the Rosary—for "without Our Lady's Help no one enters Paradise."[13]

Below is some of the other advice she offers about how to pray fully throughout the day:

Seek the Lord at Holy Mass.

"I have never enjoyed Mass and Holy Communion as much as I do here. The beautiful little church is always quiet and empty. The celebrant doesn't even have an altar boy, so I have the Lord all to myself."[14]

See and praise God in nature.

"It's marvelous on the mountain. . . . When you're up high with
the blue sky and the white snow, how can one help but rejoice
and praise God!"[15]

Make Jesus the center of your home.

"With God's help and blessing, we will do all we can to make
our new family a little cenacle where Jesus will reign over all
our affections, desires, and actions."[16]

Pray the Rosary and ask the Blessed Mother to intercede for you.

In 1955, she wrote to Pietro, "I went to Mass this morning in
our little church and I prayed to our beautiful Mother for you,
Pietro, that she would help and protect you."[17]

Have a heart filled with gratitude.

In 1958 Gianna wrote to her husband, "I go to church every
morning to thank God for all the grace he is continually giving
us."[18]

Prayer Prompt: Make an Examen

Although I like to make an Examen every night before bed, it
can be done at any time of the day, going over the past twenty-four hours of your life. Each day you will find it easier to see
the blessings in your life and to recognize your shortcomings.
Through this intentional practice of prayer, you will find great
grace and growth in your spiritual life. At each step of the
Examen exercise below, feel free to write down in your prayer
journal the thoughts that come to you.

1. Place yourself in the presence of God.

Take some deep breaths in and out and calm your mind. Imagine sitting with God.

How do you see God?

2. Give God thanks for the things in your day, naming each one.

I think of things like waking up to a new day, my health, my family, and my job, and then go into different circumstances that I have experienced throughout the day.

For what are you grateful?

3. Ask the Holy Spirit to guide you through your day to see when you were not doing God's will.

Pray ten times, "Come Holy Spirit, guide me," while taking deep breaths.

Write a prayer to the Holy Spirit.

4. Acknowledge your mistakes.

We all sin and make mistakes.

What do you regret about today?

5. Ask for forgiveness.

Ask God in your own words to forgive you for your sins. It can be difficult to say "I'm sorry," but God always extends his mercy to us.

Write a prayer of sorrow and forgiveness.

6. Make a resolution for tomorrow.

It may be something like "I will not gossip," or "I will spend five minutes in silent prayer," or "I will offer an apology to a person I have hurt today."

What is your resolution for tomorrow?

7. End with the Our Father.

CHAPTER 4

Becoming Women of Prayer
Cultivating a Legacy of Prayerfulness

Emily

Keep on doing what you have learned and received and heard and seen in me. Then the God of peace will be with you.

—Philippians 4:9

As I sat in my car waiting to pick up my son from Franciscan University for Easter break, my heart was overflowing with gratitude. More than twenty-five years ago I was there as a student, and it was then that I had the opportunity to experience what it means to be a woman of prayer. "Thank you, God, for bringing me here," I murmured as I looked across the campus, panning the landscape: the large cross on the hill, the dormitory where I lived, and the chapel where I spent many hours in prayer.

It was here at Steubenville that I had a profound spiritual experience and developed an intimate relationship with God, even as I was busy with college activities, studying and building relationships and having fun. My favorite place to find solace and peace was the tiny eucharistic adoration chapel called the Porciuncula, a replica of the church St. Francis of Assisi rebuilt in the 1200s. There in the silence I learned to hear God's voice, and those moments of prayer changed my life forever and provided me with clarity about the importance of living out an authentic relationship with Christ: in the world, but not of it.

Looking back, I am so grateful to God for bringing me there, for I almost missed the opportunity to attend Franciscan. When I was a senior in high school, my mother had prayed a novena to St. Thérèse for my vocation and for God to guide me in deciding where to go to school, what to major in, who to choose as my spouse, and most importantly, how to know God's will in my life. And yet my parents did not pressure me.

Originally I had no desire to attend this "super-Catholic school." At that time I thought prayer and church were boring, and I was sure that if I gave Jesus this yes I would end up a nun. I had not attended a Catholic school since first grade. I had yet to understand that seeking the will of God brings us the most joy. Despite all these things, God was at work in my heart, and I was filled with a new willingness to give Jesus an opportunity to lead.

I had looked at several universities, and I can still recall my college visit to another school. I bought the sweatshirt, my mom got her checkbook out to pay the deposit and enroll . . . and in those final moments, I changed my mind. I asked my mom if, instead of attending this college, I could attend Franciscan University of Steubenville, where my brother, Jonathan, was enrolled.

My mother was ecstatic at my choice, although she did not try to push my decision. She just kept praying. As we drove down a country road to visit my grandparents that same day, we came across a roadside stand selling roses. My mother had traveled that road hundreds of times but had never seen such a sight. Despite the rain falling, she gleefully pulled over and purchased a dozen red roses from the peddler to take to my grandma for her St. Thérèse statue. At the time I thought it was a bit strange, yet it wasn't until years later that my mother shared the significance of that moment. Roses are believed to be a confirmation of prayers answered through the intercession of St. Thérèse. She was thrilled that her prayer was answered. And now that beautiful statue sits in my own house and reminds me of this moment in my life as well as the faith of my mother and grandmother.

Five Things I Learned from My Family about Prayer

As I look at the legacy of prayer in my life, I see how my family has influenced my desire to grow in prayerfulness. The most influential woman in my life, the one who taught me to pray, is my mother, JoAnn. She was raised in the Catholic faith and taught us to pray as young children. When I and my siblings were very young, my mother had a sincere conversion of heart and realized the importance of a deep prayer life and personal relationship with Christ.

My dad was not Catholic in the early years of their marriage, but when my mother was in danger of another miscarriage, he realized he needed God in a powerful way. He opened his heart and began to pray. Through prayer, my father experienced a profound conversion to the Catholic faith, and in the 1980s, their marriage became rooted in prayer and their shared love for Christ through the New Evangelization.

Although I often did not want to join my mother in prayer or daily Mass when I was young, I cannot deny the impact her prayer life had on me. I still remember trying to sneak in past my curfew and seeing my mother, deep in prayer in a living room chair, praying for me and my siblings. She was always accessing God through prayer during her day, finding him in all things, and that was the fuel for her involvement in ministry work for the Church. This was attractive to me, so I slowly began to see her prayerfulness in a new light, especially when I began to grow in my own Christian faith.

My mother learned the importance of prayer from her parents, Arthur and Frances. My grandparents were simple people who were deeply committed to promoting the Sacred Heart and Immaculate Heart devotions. When my grandfather retired after thirty years of working the second shift at Ford Motor Company, he dedicated his life to making thousands upon thousands of handmade rosaries for the missions and used scrap wood to make plaques of the Sacred Heart and the Immaculate Heart of Mary in his basement. These were distributed across the world by missionary priests. One priest brought the plaques to Mother Teresa in Calcutta, who liked them so much that she began ordering them to be sent from the Cincinnati Men of the Sacred Heart to her homes for the sick and dying in India.

Who are the people in your family who have been the greatest influence on your spiritual life? What did they do that made an impression on you? Write about them at the back of this book or in your prayer journal.

As a child I enjoyed visiting my grandparents, in no small part due to the big Jimmy cake (a special cake covered in sprinkles) and other treats my grandmother would always have waiting for us. Now as an adult, I can appreciate the time we spent with our grandparents for more significant reasons. We would drive from Columbus to Cincinnati and, after two hours in the car, would jump out to join them for their favorite television program on EWTN (Eternal Word Television Network), *Mother Angelica Live*. My family would all gather on their little couch, eat snacks, and watch and learn about the faith. Then we would say the Holy Rosary.

In their front room my grandparents had two matching reclining chairs, where the two of them prayed and drank coffee every day. I found out later that they made the commitment to say all three sets of Mysteries of the Rosary daily in their retirement years, and if my grandmother didn't finish hers, my grandfather would make up for those she was lacking! Many days she would grow tired after completing one Rosary, so he would say five Rosaries to fulfill their commitment. They did all of this in addition to daily Mass and other prayers. When I was young, I thought this was just how they liked to have *fun*; now I know it was so much more than that!

My grandparents' prayers and those of my other elderly relatives grounded my mother's faith, which in turn led to the blossoming of mine. We actually used to call my great-aunt and great-uncles "The Greats" because my whole side of the family were exceptional Catholics and individuals. In many ways, I received a desire to pray and come to know Jesus as an inheritance. This wonderful inheritance of prayer is a gift I desire to pass on to my own children and future generations.

Below are five bits of advice I learned from my mother and extended family about prayer.

1. Talk to Jesus in moments of quiet.

My mother placed a picture over my bed that said, "Instead of counting sheep, why not talk to the Shepherd?" This was a great reminder to use those times I lay awake in bed to connect with Jesus. When there was silence in my home, I could focus and pour my heart out to him.

2. Spend time with Jesus in adoration.

Take time out to discover the gift of quiet and reflective prayer through eucharistic adoration. I still remember praying before

the eucharistic tabernacle as a child at Youth 2000 and feeling
the love of God flow over me. Adoration is a powerful way to
connect with Jesus and bring our joys, works, and sorrows to
him in prayer.

3. Pray with your friends.

After my parents' conversion, they looked for ways to develop
a support net through community. We hosted many youth
group meetings, prayer gatherings, and socials at our house
to grow in community through prayer. Through these events I
learned the value of hospitality and gathering others in prayer.
This was the beginning of growing my own personal prayer
life in the midst of friends.

Another of my mom's original ideas was something she
called a "Holy Spirit Potluck," where she would simply invite
a large group of friends over for prayer and tell them to bring
whatever they felt called to bring. She later told me that this
practice was less stressful than trying to coordinate the dishes
for large gatherings, and it was much easier to just leave it up
to God. Amazingly, despite zero planning, the food always
worked out.

4. Practice spontaneous prayer.

My mother often shared the intimate dialogue she was having with the Lord through the gift of spontaneous prayer. She
taught me to seek Christ in all things and at all times. She
taught me to give everything to Christ and to share his love
with others by praying together. She told me that in life you
should always offer your "roses and thorns" as intentions to
the Lord, to include Christ in the "good and bad." I learned
to pour out my heart by listening to how she prayed for each
one of her children and by seeing how the Lord was revealing
himself to her throughout her day.

5. Thank the Lord.

My mom taught me to always have joy and be grateful for all God does. My mom's gratitude is best expressed in her willingness to show hospitality to others and her love for the faith that always leads to action. She notices the promptings of the Spirit and acts on them. She thanks the Lord continually for his many blessings and offers prayers of thanks by saying novenas and lighting candles at church. She loves to share with others the joy and excitement that comes from living a life rooted in prayer and following in Christ's footsteps. Thanks to the solid spiritual foundation I received from my mom, I have learned to appreciate the gift of prayer and desire to pass it on to others.

The Gift of Spiritual Community

Developing an authentic relationship with Christ and gathering with like-minded believers in community are essential for becoming a woman of prayer. St. John Paul II once said, "Our Christian communities must become *genuine* 'schools' of prayer, where the meeting with Christ is expressed not just in imploring help but also in thanksgiving, praise, adoration, contemplation, listening and ardent devotion, until the heart truly 'falls in love.' . . . By opening our heart to the love of God it also opens it to the love of our brothers and sisters, and makes us capable of shaping history according to God's plan."[1]

We are called to be sincere in our prayer life and to experience the gift of faith through an authentic love of God, and to share that with others. When we are genuine, others can receive an authentic faith experience.

Over the years, I have learned firsthand the impact of having faith-filled friends and community involved in my life as a source of strength. Spiritual friendships have been a key in my own spiritual awakening and love for the Catholic faith. Advancing in the spiritual life can be difficult, especially when you don't have a support system. Looking back, I have come to appreciate that many pivotal moments in my own faith journey were experienced alongside good friends. When I was a teenager, a friend invited me to attend a retreat for the first time; I joined a prayer group in my twenties and a Bible study group in my thirties. When I reached my forties, I began working in women's ministry with a group of faith-filled women in my city, and began writing, speaking, and sharing my faith with others—and having Michele working alongside me always made it better.

St. Teresa of Avila once said, "I would counsel those who practice prayer to seek, at least in the beginning, friendship and association with other persons having the same interest . . . even though the association may be only to help one another with prayers. The more of the prayers there are, the greater the gain." She went on to explain that spiritual friendships are so important, "I do not know how to urge it enough. . . . It is necessary for those who serve Him to become shields for one another that they might advance."[2]

Sturdy, faith-filled friends are essential to help us withstand the storms in our lives and provide support when we need it. The process of deepening and developing these relationships is well worth the time and effort required, and these friendships can blossom into our greatest treasures in life. The road to sanctification is always easier to travel with others by your side. Spiritual friendship is a priceless gift that helps us become the women of prayer we long to be.

Who are the spiritual friends who have meant the most to you, and why? Where do you find a community of support to help you grow in your faith? Record your thoughts in your prayer journal.

Let's Pray: "Love One Another"

In the Gospel of John, we find Jesus in the Upper Room at the Last Supper, where he teaches his disciples: "I give you a new commandment: love one another. As I have loved you, so you also should love one another. This is how all will know that you are my disciples, if you have love for one another" (Jn 13:34–35).

Let us pause and pray on this scripture. Invite Jesus into your heart and ask him how he would like you to share his love with others. What was Jesus saying to you, as you read these words from the Last Supper account?

Who needs you to show them love the most in their life right now? How can you do that best?

How can you continue the legacy of faith in your own family or greater community? Write down your thoughts.

Meet Your Heavenly Friends: Sts. Louis and Zélie Martin

Imagine what it would be like if your children said about you what St. Thérèse said about her parents: "The Good God gave me a father and mother more worthy of Heaven than of earth."[3]

Sts. Louis and Zélie Martin were the parents of St. Thérèse of Lisieux, "the Little Flower," the great Doctor of the Church. They were not canonized because of their daughter, however; they were recognized for the authentic Catholic Christian life they lived. "Louis and Zélie Martin are sublime examples of conjugal love, of an industrious Christian family concerned for others, generous to the poor and inspired by an exemplary missionary spirit, ever ready to help with parish activities."[4] They hold the distinction of being the first married couple with children canonized together during the same ceremony, as well as being the parents of one of the most influential saints in modern times.[5]

Both members of this remarkable couple thought they would enter the religious life, yet they joyfully responded to the call to marriage. They lived through difficult trials, and yet they always had faith and courage to seek Christ. Zélie died at age forty-five from breast cancer when Thérèse was only four years old. She left behind a legacy of faith, courage, industry, and a deeply devoted prayer life.

Louis Martin (1823–1894) was initially destined to serve in the French military, but in his early twenties he decided to pursue a religious vocation at the monastery of the Augustinian canons of the Great St. Bernard in the Alps. His struggles with Latin hindered him, and he eventually took on the career of a skilled watchmaker instead. He settled in the small French city of Alençon. There he met Zélie Guerin (1831–1877), who also longed for the religious life.[6] One day while praying about her future and her desire to support herself, Zélie heard an inner voice say, "Undertake the making of point d'Alençon lace."[7] She went on to master the Alençon lace-making technique, a desired fashion of the time, and established a profitable center for making this lace.

Zélie discovered her husband in much the same way. As she was crossing the St. Leonard's bridge, her path crossed with that of her future spouse. *"That is he whom I have prepared for you,"* she heard a voice say.[8] In July 1858 they married, Zélie twenty-seven and Louis thirty-six.

Louis the watchmaker and Zélie the lace maker became the parents of nine children, five of whom survived to adulthood. This couple showed tremendous courage in embracing their vocation and seeking the will of God in all things during their fifteen years of marriage. They share in their letters how their children were their greatest joy and that their one desire as a couple was to be saints in heaven with their children.

The Martins' active prayer life included attending 5:30 a.m. Mass together, assisting at solemn high Mass and at Vespers, saying morning and evening prayers as well as grace before meals, and following a regular practice of fasting.

Louis and Zélie were beatified on October 19, 2008, and were canonized by Pope Francis on October 18, 2015. The liturgical feast of Sts. Louis Martin and Zélie Guerin is July 12. Through the 218 letters written by Zélie, and sixteen more from Louis, we gain vast insight into the spiritual life they shared and the daily joys, sorrows, and trials they experienced.

Sts. Zélie and Louis Martin, pray for us!

Passing On a Legacy of Prayer: Advice from St. Zélie Martin

Zélie's words of courage and faith give us hope as we endure long days at work, the trials of parenting, and the challenges of living our faith in our modern culture. St. Zélie offers us a personal perspective on the power of prayer, service, and love, even in difficult times.

She once wrote, "I often think of my saintly sister and of her quiet, peaceful life [in the convent]. She works, but not to gain perishable riches; she is active only for Heaven, which she is ever looking forward to and longing for. As for me, I see myself bent towards the earth, toiling with all my strength to amass gold which I cannot take with me, and which I have no desire to take. . . . Sometimes I regret that I did not become a nun like her, but immediately I say to myself, 'But I would not have my four little girls, and my darling Joseph! No! It is better for me to toil on, as I am, and to have them with me.'"[9]

With the help of Christ, Zélie embraced the joys and sorrows of her vocation as wife and mother. For all of us, Zélie offers valuable advice on living the Christian life well:

Accept the cross that God has chosen for you.

"We have to carry our cross in one way or another. We say to God, 'I do not want this one.' Often our prayer is heard, but often, also, to our own misfortune. It's better to patiently accept what happens to us. There is always joy alongside the pain."[10]

Pray for courage to accept God's will even when life is difficult.

Zélie was accepting even of the cancer that took her from her young children. Her final words were, "If the Blessed Virgin does not cure me, it is because my time is done and the good God wants me to rest somewhere other than on earth."[11]

Look for opportunities to witness to God's goodness to others.

"The good Lord fits the back for the burden, and never asks more than we could bear. Very often I have seen my husband worried about my health, while I could not have been calmer. I used to say to him: 'Don't be afraid; the good God is with us!' I had, though, loads of work and preoccupations, but I felt that firm confidence of being always helped by Heaven."[12]

Pray you will become a saint.

"I want to become a saint; it will not be easy at all. I have a lot of wood to chop and it is as hard as stone. I should have started sooner, while it was not so difficult; but in any case, 'better late than never.'"[13]

Keep a careful watch over your children's faith life.

Over and over again, St. Zélie shared that her children were her everything, and it was her goal to raise them to know, love, and serve God. She was attentive to her children and helped them to grow in the love of God. In their letters, St. Thérèse's sisters wrote, "Mamma carefully watched over us, and kept away from us even the shadow of evil."[14]

Prayer Prompt: Pray for a Legacy of Faith

At some time in our lives, we all face the prospect of carrying burdens or enduring hardship—including difficulties that, from a purely human perspective, seem too much for us. Jesus says that we are to come to him with these burdens and give them to him so that we can find rest: "For my yoke is easy, and my burden light" (Mt 11:30).

To begin, close your eyes and open your heart and mind to the Lord. Place yourself in the presence of God, and reflect on the many blessings, joys, and sorrows that fill your days, and how his love is a constant source of strength.

Now think about those friends and loved ones whose spiritual legacy has left a lasting imprint on your faith life. Offer up prayers of thanksgiving for these people that have shared, inspired, and passed on the important legacy of prayer.

Who has inspired you to become a stronger woman of prayer? How can you pass on a legacy of prayer to others? Reflect on these questions in your prayer journal.

Tell Jesus where you need courage in your life. Ask him to help you embrace your daily crosses and struggles.

Write a prayer, asking Jesus to help you in the specific areas of your life where you feel you most need to cultivate courage.

After thanking the Lord for the faith legacy that you have received, and sharing your prayer petitions for courage, read and reflect on the following passage: "Peace I leave with you;

my peace I give to you. Not as the world gives do I give it to
you. Do not let your hearts be troubled or afraid" (Jn 14:27).

What strikes you about this passage? Write down your thoughts.

Close with a short prayer thanking God for his many blessings.
Thank Jesus for this time you spent together. Ask Jesus to help
you grow closer to him each day and to have courage to live
out his will in your life.

CHAPTER 5

Hello, Is Anyone Listening?
The Mystery of Unanswered Prayer

Michele

Every woman, in the way most suitable to her, should try
to find "breathing spaces"—moments in which she can
return to herself and rest in God.

—Edith Stein

I was lying in my bed one evening when a text from my aunt
Rose came in: "Please pray for Uncle Mike, he's had a small
stroke." I was shocked; my uncle was only fifty-seven years old
and in good health. An avid outdoorsman and photographer,
he didn't have any of the risk factors typically associated with
stroke. I told my husband and our family, sent out emails to
all my prayer chains, then sat down and prayed.

At first, things were positive. The stroke provided a reason
for unexplained health issues Uncle Mike had been having in
prior weeks. Aunt Rose text-messaged me regular updates. My
uncle went into inpatient rehab and insisted that Aunt Rose
go on her planned pilgrimage to Medjugorje, a place where

apparitions of the Blessed Mother have reportedly been occurring since 1981. The trip now had a new meaning and purpose, a place for Aunt Rose to pray for Mike's complete healing.

While away on her pilgrimage, Rose received status reports on Mike's condition. He was responding to physical and occupational therapy; he even ran down the hallway, bouncing a basketball. Then, on her final day of the trip, Mike started having seizures. He was moved to Barnes-Jewish Hospital, a research hospital in St. Louis, Missouri, to be treated. There he was diagnosed with Creutzfeldt-Jakob disease (CJD), a rare, degenerative, fatal brain disorder.

A miracle was their only hope. Aunt Rose told me, "I had him put on every prayer list I knew of, I even called religious orders and asked them for prayers for a miracle. The hospital room was filled with holy oils, holy water, images of Jesus and relics of saints lined up on the windowsill. We prayed the Chaplet of Divine Mercy and the Rosary at his bedside. We asked everyone we knew to pray the 'Miracle Prayer' written by Fr. Rookey and asking his intercession, along with all the saints and angels."

Despite everything, Mike's condition grew worse. After only two weeks at the hospital, he was moved to hospice, and passed away with his son at his side less than twenty-four hours after being admitted.

Although it was devastating to my aunt that her prayers were not answered as she'd hoped, she still saw God's hand at work. "I did not receive what I asked for, but we did receive answers to many other prayers," she said. "For two years I had been praying with my youngest son that Mike would go to confession. I knew he had not gone since he became Catholic more than thirty years ago. My prayer was also that it would not be on his deathbed, but God had other plans."

In the hospital, Mike willingly received the Anointing of the Sick, which gives special graces: "uniting . . . the sick person to the passion of Christ, for his own good and that of the whole

Church; the strengthening, peace, and courage to endure in a Christian manner the sufferings of illness or old age; *the forgiveness of sins, if the sick person was not able to obtain it through the sacrament of penance*; the restoration of health, if it is conducive to the salvation of his soul; the preparation for passing over to eternal life" (*CCC*, 1532, emphasis mine).

Aunt Rose went on to share that God had also given her many consolations. One in particular had personal meaning for her. As a natural light photographer, Mike had taken a snapshot of a beautiful blue butterfly that had landed on their daughter Christina. "Before he died, I asked Mike to share with me a sign in nature when he was with God," Rose said. That fall, at the wedding of a friend's daughter, Rose arrived early and decided to pray the Rosary with her daughter and a friend for the couple's marriage. "As soon as we started the Rosary, a pretty gray and blue butterfly sat on my leg and rested. I couldn't help but notice that the gray of the butterfly matched my dress exactly, and the blue was the same shade as the crystal beads of my rosary."

The butterfly stayed on her lap until the end of the Rosary, but as soon as they concluded with the Sign of the Cross, it flew away. "I took that as a sign Mike was with God and joining us in prayer. He really wanted to be at that wedding, and at that moment, he was."

Another consolation that God sent Rose's way came in the form of financial assistance. "Mike was the breadwinner in the family and took care of all the home maintenance, car repairs, and many of the daily tasks around the house. After his death, friends, neighbors, and family came to help us. For two months meals were brought every other day. They made many repairs on our home, completely rebuilt the deck, and replaced the kitchen faucets." A year later, people were still coming and helping. "God provided whatever I was lacking through the help of my friends. They were the hands and feet of Christ to me in my time of need."

I asked Aunt Rose for some practical tips on prayer. The most important, she said, was to develop a prayer life *before* a crisis hits. "When you are in crisis, it's really hard to pray," she told me. "Even though I had a deep prayer life before I lost Mike, after his death I struggled. I went to Mass every week, but I couldn't pray or go into quiet time with the Lord for many months. I was too grief stricken, I couldn't sit in the quiet, I needed distraction. However, after months of healing, I was able to get back into my prayer routine: going to Mass on my day off, spending time with Jesus in adoration, and praying the Rosary. I didn't feel anything at first—I just kept plugging along. I knew the shock and numbness would go away. I just did what I could, even if it was mechanical prayer, and I persevered. I knew it was the only way to get through all of this."

How did suffering such a great loss impact her prayer life? "I still want my will," my aunt said. "But I have learned to surrender and accept even the answer I really didn't want. It wasn't easy; I went through shock, anger, and disbelief. It's still hard for me to grapple with the fact that he was alive and walking around and now he is gone. Acceptance has taken time, but I do have peace.

"As I continue on my journey on earth," she concluded, "I look at prayer through a different lens. When I pray, I remind myself, 'I am going to ask God for this—but I know he is going to give me what is according to *his* will.' I learned that real prayer leads to complete surrender and trust in God. Before this, I would beg and plead for the answer I wanted from God. Now I look at conforming to his will."

Ask and You Shall Receive?

Why doesn't God always give us what we ask? Why did Angel (in chapter 1) get the healing she needed and my uncle did not? The reality is that most of us can probably relate a great deal more to the second story, the story of suffering and loss. All of us have asked for that miracle that never came: a healing, a job, or some material thing. Often we do not receive the answer we wanted.

Can you remember a time when you asked and did not receive what you wanted? Did any good come out of this unanswered prayer? Write down your thoughts in your prayer journal.

And yet the scriptures are clear; we are to ask for what we need: "And I tell you, ask and you will receive; seek and you will find; knock and the door will be opened to you. For everyone who asks, receives; and the one who seeks, finds; and to the one who knocks, the door will be opened" (Lk 11:9–10).

So often as we knock we are also wondering, "Is God really listening?" When we don't get what we ask for, we even blame him for what is happening to us. "Why, God? Why me? Why my family? Why suffering?" It can be so hard for us to understand how God, who is a good God and loves us, would let bad things happen to us.

It's okay to feel that way and to talk to God about it. When we are in relationship with God, our prayers can be real, honest, and even raw. One of my favorite, eye-opening books about prayer was written by a priest named Fr. Jim Willig, who suffered a long time with renal cancer and shared his journey in *Lessons from the School of Suffering*.

Fr. Jim relays a time when his treatments were not working and he went to the Lord in prayer. "I said things like, 'Do you really care about me?' . . . 'Does it even matter to you that thousands of people are praying for me?'" As he continued to pray from the heart, he went on to say, "I was angry and I told Jesus things that I never thought I could say, because it was, indeed, everything I felt. Everything—the good, the bad, and the ugly. It was as if I was throwing up. It just kept coming. I told God things that I had never before *known* I even felt.

"This went on for two hours! I honestly thought my eyes would run out of tears. Only then could I manage to stop long enough to ask, 'So, Lord, do you have anything to say for yourself?' What came into my mind was that the Lord was responding to me by saying, 'Yes. You need to take a break. Then come back and we can continue this conversation.'"[1]

Later in prayer, Fr. Jim felt God lead him to read the Emmaus story in scripture, and he stopped short on a particular verse that resonated within him: "Did you not understand that you had to undergo all of this so as to enter into my glory?" (see Luke 24:26).

How have you experienced the truth of this passage in your life? Write down your thoughts.

Fr. Jim then understood that the Lord knew that the best way for him to be sanctified was through suffering, "this way of the cross, this cross of cancer."[2] Reading this story helped me see that if a holy priest could talk to God in this very sincere and heartfelt way, then I too needed to be open with God in all that I was thinking and feeling in my heart if I wanted to be in true relationship with him.

It is impossible with our finite minds to grasp the greater, all-encompassing view that God has of our life. It's like we are working on a tiny corner of a million-piece puzzle. We want everything to fit just so, and when it doesn't, we groan in pain. Yet if we could only look up from our little corner to see the grand masterpiece that God has planned for us, even the most difficult times would blend in on our great journey of life to make a gorgeous sight for us to behold.

Prayer is our anchor. It secures us in God during the difficult moments. As we journey through hard times, we grow and learn to be more reliant on him. Like my aunt Rose in her journey, we also realize that everyone suffers and has trials.

Each and every day, we are faced with some sort of challenge. Through these sufferings, we come to learn that God's grace will carry us through. God uses these trials to help us grow in holiness, and it is prayer that gives us the strength to endure the difficult times.

Fr. Jacques Philippe writes, "Thanks to a regular encounter with God in prayer, everything, in the end, becomes positive: our desires, our good will, our efforts, but also our poverty, our errors, our sins. Our fortunate or unfortunate circumstances, good or bad choices—everything is 'summed up' in Christ and becomes grace. Everything winds up making sense and is integrated into a path of growth through love."[3]

Let's Pray: Remember God's Goodness

One way to keep perspective on how God is working in your life is to journal times of answered prayers. Then, when you are going through a difficult time, you can read and be consoled.

Can you think of a time God answered a prayer for you? Write a prayer of gratitude in response.

What about a time that your prayers were not answered? Talk to God about how that made you feel, or write him a note.

Did God answer your prayer in an unexpected way, or reveal himself to you in your difficulty? If you cannot see God's hand during this time, ask him to show you. Write down your thoughts.

At the back of this book there is a place for you to write down prayer intentions and reflections on how God has worked in your life. Take time each night to jot down when good things happen, so they can remind you of God's love and care for you.

Meet Your Heavenly Friend:
Edith Stein (St. Teresa Benedicta of the Cross)

Over the years I have grown to learn about and love many saintly friends, who have gone before us to heaven yet are still part of our lives. One of my favorite modern-day saints is Edith Stein, a woman of deep prayer who converted from the Jewish faith and, in seeking the truth, became a Carmelite nun.

Edith was born to Auguste and Siegfried Stein on October 12, 1891, in Breslau, Germany, on the feast of Yom Kippur. She was the youngest of seven surviving children. Her family was committed to the practice of Jewish prayer and worship. When Edith was two, her father suddenly passed away due to heatstroke, leaving her mother to run the family lumber business and raise the children.

When Edith was fourteen years old, she made a conscious decision to leave her Jewish faith and became an atheist. She excelled in her academic studies and was one of the first women in Germany to go to college. At the university, Edith focused on literature, philosophy, and history. Through her studies, she came to know the truth of Christianity and develop a true understanding of the identity of women. Edith went on to complete her doctoral work; however, she was not allowed to become a university professor because she was a woman.

As her academic career was unfolding, Edith became severely depressed. Although she desired to overcome it by an act of will, she realized this was a wall that would not give. She wrote, "It reached a point where life seemed unbearable. I couldn't cross the street without hoping to be run over or go hiking without wanting to fall so that I wouldn't have to come back alive. Nobody had the least idea of what was going on inside of me."[4]

In 1921, Edith read *The Book of Her Life* by St. Teresa of Avila and was profoundly impacted by its truth. She converted to

Catholicism in 1922. During this time in her life, she worked as a teacher and became a popular lecturer. She was a professional woman in the work world, yet her faith drew her into deep prayer. She wrote, "Every woman, in the way most suitable to her, should try to find 'breathing spaces'—moments in which she can return to herself and rest in God."[5] Edith placed great importance on taking time out for private retreats and pilgrimages.

Edith accepted a position as a lecturer at the German Institute of Scientific Pedagogy, but after only a year, as the influence of Nazism spread across Germany, her position was terminated. The loss of her career opened the door for her to follow her desire to seek a vocation as a Carmelite nun; in 1933, she entered the Carmel of Cologne.

In the convent, Edith continued to write, especially on the redemptive power of suffering and the importance of uniting one's own suffering with that of Christ on the Cross. She offered her own sufferings for an end to the terrible evils of her time and the holocaust of the Jewish people. Edith was transferred to a convent in Echt, Holland, when Germany became too dangerous for her, but in 1942, the Nazi police arrested all Jewish converts to Christianity and sent them to concentration camps. Edith and her sister Rosa traveled with many religious from the area to Auschwitz-Birkenau. On August 9, 1942, she was gassed and burned before even entering the camp. She is honored in the Catholic Church as a martyr.[6]

The Gift of Redemptive Suffering: Advice from St. Edith Stein

When Edith took the name Sr. Teresa Benedicta and entered the Carmel, her total change of heart was not understood or accepted by those who loved her. Her mother cried when Edith told her the news: "Why did you get to know it [Christianity]?

I don't want to say anything against [Christ]. He may have been a very good person. But why did he make himself God?"[7]

The purity of her motives was not accepted by her enemies, who continued to seek her life—and did not stop until she and her sister Rosa, who had also converted and resided in the same convent, were murdered in the gas chambers of Auschwitz. And yet, Edith saw even in this a kind of glory ahead: "I ask the Lord to accept my life and my death . . . so that the Lord will be accepted by His people and that His Kingdom may come in glory, for the salvation of Germany and the peace of the world."[8]

Despite the hardships, through her conversion Edith found the peace she had been seeking all her life. Within the cloistered life, she was able to take time away from the distractions of the world to focus on her interior life. And so, this convert martyr saint has much to teach those who struggle to understand and accept the will of God. Here are some of the things we can learn from her example.

Have a quiet place to pray.

"The only essential is that one finds, first of all, a quiet corner in which one can communicate with God as though there were nothing else, and that must be done daily."[9]

Give your first waking moments to the Lord.

"The duties and cares for the day ahead crowd about us when we awake in the morning (if they have not already dispelled our night's rest). Now arises the uneasy question: How can all this be accommodated in one day? When will I do this, when that? How shall I start this and that? Thus agitated, we would like to run around and rush forth. We must take the reins in hand and say, 'Take it easy,' not any of this may touch me now. My first morning's hour belongs to the Lord. I will tackle the day's work which he charges me with, and he will give me the power to accomplish it."[10]

Take a break midday to spend time with the Lord.

"It is the noon hour. . . . Each one must know, or get to know, where and how she may find peace. The best way, when it is possible, is to shed all cares again for a short time before the tabernacle . . . and . . . if pressing duties prevent a quiet hour, then she must for a moment seal off herself inwardly against all things and take refuge in the Lord. He is indeed there and can give us in a single moment all we need."[11]

At the end of the day, lay all that is undone in the hands of the Lord.

"When night comes, and retrospect shows that everything was patchwork and much one has planned has been left undone, when so many things rouse shame and regret, then take all as it is, lay it in God's hands, and offer it up to Him. In this way we will be able to rest in Him, actually to rest, and to begin the new day like a new life."[12]

Always live in the presence of God.

"There's quite a distance between leading the self-satisfied existence of the 'good Catholic' who 'does his duty,' 'reads the right newspaper' and 'votes correctly'—and then does just as he pleases—and living one's life in the presence of God, with the simplicity of a child and humility of the publican. But I can assure you: once anyone has taken the first step, he won't want to turn back."[13]

Prayer Prompt:
"I Am Always in Your Midst"

Edith Stein found poetry a beautiful outlet for prayer. Let us reflect together on a poem she wrote. Take a few deep breaths, in through your nose and out through your mouth. Place yourself in the presence of God. Slowly read through each line of the poem below.

> **"I Am Always in Your Midst"**
> Of course, the Lord leads each on her own path,
> And what we call "fate"; is the artist's doing,
> The eternal Artist, who creates material for
>   himself
> And forms it into images in various ways:
> By gentle finger strokes and also by chisel
>   blows.
> But he does not work on dead material;
> His greatest creative joy in fact is
> That under his hand the image stirs,
> That life pours forth to meet him.
> That life that he himself has placed in it
> And that now answers him from within
> To chisel blows or quiet finger strokes.
> So we collaborate with God on his work of art.[14]

Which words spoke to you as you read this poem? Write them in your journal.

Now think of a time when you felt God molding you gently.

Do you believe you are a beautiful work of art created by God? How does that make you feel? Journal your thoughts.

Write a poem or letter to God in response to reading this poem. Some questions you may ponder:

   What do you feel called to say?
   What are you afraid of?
   What is holding you back from sitting in God's loving embrace?
   What crosses are you carrying?
   What joys are in your heart?
   What are you thankful for?
   What do you want to ask God for?

CHAPTER 6

Prayer Protections
Devotions to Draw Us
Deeper into Prayer

Emily

Whenever this sacred image [of the Sacred Heart of Jesus]
would be exposed for veneration He would pour forth His
graces and blessings.

—St. Margaret Mary Alacoque [1]

In 2014, we dedicated our home to the Sacred Heart of Jesus
through the enthronement and consecration to the Sacred
Heart. We welcomed Jesus as King, Savior, and friend to be
present in our house, and as a family we placed the images of
the Sacred Heart of Jesus and the Immaculate Heart of Mary
on our mantel.

For generations, my extended family on my mother's side
has had a devotion to the Sacred Heart. This image, a sign of
Christ's love burning for mankind, was displayed in each of

their homes and brought comfort to our family during difficult times. I felt drawn to the devotion from the first time I heard of St. Margaret Mary, the French mystic who received visitations of Our Lord from 1673 to 1675.

At the time we dedicated our home, we didn't have any pressing issues for which we felt we needed special graces, but we recognized that any help the Lord could offer would be a welcome blessing in the life of our family. We had six children from age fourteen on down, and we were always on the move, driving to and from school, sports, and other activities. Anything that could bring us all together to pray and grow closer to God would be a huge bonus.

A week or so after our enthronement of the Sacred Heart, I called down to my son who was in the basement working out. "Come up for dinner. We are ready to eat." At first there was no response. I knew in my gut that something was wrong. Just minutes before, my strong and athletic eighth grader was on the treadmill exercising and now the basement was silent. After calling again, I heard a quiet, sleepy response, "I'm too tired to eat. I think I'm going to take a nap." I quickly went downstairs and found my son curled up on the floor. I began to pray silently to the Sacred Heart to reveal what was wrong.

"What's the matter?" I asked him. He replied, "I don't know, all of a sudden I just got so tired." I urged him to get up, and we went upstairs. Soon after he began to perk up. As I continued praying in my head, two words came to me in a flash of clarity: carbon monoxide! The next day we had our basement checked and, sure enough, found out that both our furnace and water heater were not venting properly; our basement had extremely high levels of the dangerous gas. I continue to thank God that we discovered this serious risk to which we were being slowly exposed, and I give full credit to the protection of Jesus' Sacred Heart.

The technician who put in our new furnace kept saying we were so "lucky" based on how high our readings were, but I knew it wasn't luck. It was a blessing and protection given by the Sacred Heart, and it didn't stop there. Since the enthronement, I have come to appreciate when our children need extra attention and emotional support, and I bring these intentions along with my other needs to his holy heart. Jesus offers us not only physical protection but spiritual protection as well. Our Lord wants us to turn to him for daily strength and safety and to expose the areas of our life that need extra attention.

The Sacred Heart of Jesus devotion gives us graces, blessings, hope, healing, and spiritual protection. St. Margaret Mary shared that, "as to persons living in the world, they shall find in this amiable devotion all the aids necessary in their state of life; that is to say, peace in the homes, consolation in their work, the blessings of heaven upon all their enterprises, comfort in their sorrow, a secure refuge during life and especially at the hour of death."[2] When we honor the heart of Christ, we welcome perfect love into our hearts, which blots out all evil and teaches us how to live a life rooted in Christ.

Gradually, after the enthronement, we began to turn more to Jesus for our daily needs and see the value of welcoming Jesus into our lives on a more personal level. Our family continues to have a full plate, but we have been given new graces to live out our faith and receive spiritual protection. "This devotion was a last effort of His love which wishes to favor men in these last centuries with this loving redemption, in order to withdraw them from the empire of Satan, which He intended to destroy, and in order to put us under the sweet empire of His love. This He would establish in the hearts of all those who embrace this devotion."[3]

The Lord constantly desires to reveal what we need to know and to equip us for our journey. Each morning, I pray before my image of the Sacred Heart and ask the Lord to protect me and my entire family from evil. The gift of enthronement of the Sacred Heart is offered to all Catholics to strengthen families and provide a lifeline of grace.

How Do Devotions Enrich Us?

Devotions are meant to draw us into deeper prayer. The Church has numerous special devotions to the saints, the angels, the Blessed Mother, and to Jesus, such as Divine Mercy and the Sacred Heart.

According to the United States Conference of Catholic Bishops, "Popular devotional practices play a crucial role in helping to foster this ceaseless prayer. The faithful have always used a variety of practices as a means of permeating everyday life with prayer to God. Examples include pilgrimages, novenas, processions and celebrations in honor of Mary and the other saints, the Rosary, the Angelus, the Stations of the Cross, the veneration of relics, and the use of sacramentals. Properly used, popular devotional practices do not replace the liturgical life of the Church; rather, they extend it into daily life."[4]

These devotions lead us to Christ and serve as catalysts for the grace we need to transform our lives and resist temptation. Getting to know the *why* behind these devotions leaves us with a stronger faith and a clearer picture of the role they play in the life of our faith. Pope Pius XII writes that the purpose of devotionals is "to attract and direct our souls to God, purifying them from their sins, encouraging them to practice virtue and, finally, stimulating them to advance along the path of sincere piety by accustoming them to meditate on the eternal truths and disposing them better to contemplate the mysteries of the human and divine natures of Christ."[5]

Sanctifying Sacramentals

"Why do you wear that medal of Mary around your neck?" Have you been asked this question? Many of us wear religious items but may not exactly know why. Perhaps we wear them because they identify us as Catholic, but the reality is they do so much more than that!

Holy medals and other sacramentals help us grow closer and stay close to Jesus. The *Catechism* teaches, "Sacramentals do not confer the grace of the Holy Spirit in the way that the sacraments do, but by the Church's prayer, they prepare us to receive grace and dispose us to cooperate with it. For well-disposed members of the faithful, the liturgy of the sacraments and sacramentals sanctifies almost every event of their lives with the divine grace which flows from the Paschal Mystery of the Passion, Death, and Resurrection of Christ. From this source all sacraments and sacramentals draw their power" (1670).

Our homes are meant to be places of prayer, and sacramentals—including holy Christian images—are meant to draw us into prayer. I have found that each time I walk past my Sacred Heart image hanging in my front room or notice a rosary on my end table, it invites me to pray. Jesus' most Sacred Heart is the perfect reminder that he loves us and wants to develop a meaningful relationship with us through prayer.

Take a brief look around your house. Do you have any holy images that point to God in your home? Are they in a place of prominence to serve as a reminder to pause and pray?

Let's Pray: Visio Divina

One powerful and healing type of meditative prayer is called *visio divina,* or "divine seeing." Visio divina allows you to contemplate God and pray through sacred images. You can use any holy image as a focal point and gaze upon it. Let's take a moment to ponder this beautiful image of Jesus' Sacred Heart.[6]

Now place yourself in God's presence and take a few deep breaths.

Read the following scripture:

> For I am convinced that neither death, nor life, nor angels, nor principalities, nor present things, nor future things, nor powers, nor height, nor depth, nor any other creature will be able to separate us from the love of God in Christ Jesus our Lord. (Rom 8:38–39)

As you think about these questions, write down your thoughts in your prayer journal or the back of this book:

* Gaze upon the image of Jesus with his hand on his heart. What strikes you about this image?
* Gaze upon the image again and spend a moment in silence. What do you see this time? How is God speaking to you?
* Gaze upon the image a third time and spend a moment in silence. Allow God to lead you in prayer.

Close with a prayer of thanksgiving. Offer a simple prayer such as, "Dear Lord, thank you for this time we spent together meditating on your love for me. Thank you for the special graces, blessings, hope, and healing you give to us through your Sacred Heart."

Many different items can become sacramentals through a blessing provided by Catholic deacons, priests, or bishops. These items include sacred art, icons, rosaries, medals, scapulars, and religious statues. It is important to show these holy items respect and know that they can assist you in your spiritual journey toward becoming a woman of prayer.

What about the Rosary?

One of my favorite devotions is the Holy Rosary. The Rosary is more than praying multiple Hail Marys, Our Fathers, and

Glory Bes; it is an opportunity to meditate on the life of Christ and the Blessed Mother. As I read each Mystery of the Rosary, I imagine the scene and place myself in in it—witnessing the event firsthand with Jesus, Mary, and the apostles. (If you are unfamiliar with the Mysteries, there are numerous books, websites, and apps that can help you meditate on the scenes.)

The Rosary is a particularly "Marian" devotion—that is, it is focused on the life of Mary and her experiences as the Mother of God. But remember that the Blessed Mother will always guide us closer to her son. Jesus declares from the Cross, "Behold, your mother" (Jn 19:27). These powerful words remind us that Jesus wants us to invite Mary into our life as our mother so that she may lead us to him. "The figure of Mary guides us on our way . . . to her we confidently entrust ourselves."[7]

We gain special graces by praying the Holy Rosary and meditating on the life of Christ. It helps us to grow in virtue and reject vice.[8] When we pray the Rosary in a quiet place, the meditative rhythm can calm us and prepare us to enter into deeper prayer. A priest friend of ours, Fr. Daniel Swartz, shared that "God uses rhythm to touch our hearts and draw us into a more intimate level with him."

Dr. Edward Sri writes, "The Rosary can take us deeper—a lot deeper. . . . It enables us to rest in God's presence. It draws out the deepest desires in our souls, desire for God and God alone."[9] Many times when I pray the Rosary, I play quiet, meditative music in the background. If you search "rosary music" on the Internet, you will find several selections from which to choose.

You don't have to pray the whole Rosary at once. It's not an "all or none" type of prayer. If you only have a few minutes, it's okay to say just one or two decades. I have discovered that it is better to pray only one decade slowly, meditating on the Mystery, calling out to Jesus each time you say his name, rather than rush through the whole thing. The Holy Rosary is a prayer that we can place all our confidence in, knowing that Our Lady is ever present when we take time out to meditate on the life of Our Lord.

Meet Your Heavenly Friend: St. Margaret Mary Alacoque

St. Margaret Mary Alacoque, also known as the "Apostle of the Sacred Heart," experienced the tremendous gift of developing an intimate relationship with Jesus' Most Sacred Heart. His heart became her source of protection and fount of all love and inspiration to seek profound holiness.

St. Margaret Mary was born in the Diocese of Autun, France, on July 22, 1647. She was the fifth of seven children. Even as a child, she had a deep love for the Lord and was devoted to Our Lady, his mother.

At the age of nine, she made her first Holy Communion. "This Communion shed such bitterness over all my little pleasures and amusements that I was no longer able to enjoy any of them, although I sought them eagerly."[10]

After this she became extremely ill: "I fell into so pitiable a state of ill health that for about four years I was unable to walk. My bones pierced my skin . . . since no remedy could be found for my illness, I was consecrated to the Blessed Virgin with the promise that, if she cured me, I should one day be one of her daughters."[11] She was cured, and in 1671, she joined the Visitation order at Paray-le-Monial and was professed the following year.

St. Margaret Mary experienced visions of Christ himself, who revealed his most Sacred Heart to her and his deep love for mankind. All the visions occurred while St. Margaret Mary was praying before the Blessed Sacrament or after receiving Holy Communion. Sometimes his heart was a blazing furnace, while at other times it was torn and bleeding because of the coldness and sin of mankind.

She saw Christ's heart engulfed in flames and surrounded by thorns and heard his loving voice share these words, "Behold this Heart, which has loved so much but has received nothing but coldness, indifference, and ingratitude in return."[12] St. Margaret Mary knew Christ had selected her and, with the help of Fr. Claude de La Colombière of the Society of Jesus, was instrumental in instituting the great feast of the Sacred Heart and spreading devotion to the Sacred Heart throughout the world.

Through the Sacred Heart of Jesus devotion, we allow Christ to renew us and transform our own hearts. St. Margaret Mary Alacoque revealed to us not only a devotion that the world desperately needs but also a roadmap to holiness through loving the heart of Christ. This saint shared the messages of Christ in a way that touched even the hardest of sinners and provided many with hope that miracles can happen when hearts unite with Christ. St. Margaret Mary died on October 17, 1690, at the age of forty-two and was canonized on May 13, 1920, by Pope Benedict XV.[13]

Draw Close to the Heart of Jesus: Advice from St. Margaret Mary Alacoque

We can learn a lot from the words shared by St. Margaret Mary Alacoque on loving the heart of Christ.

Seek the Giver, not just his gifts.

"As for the other graces and gifts I receive from His bounty, I must confess that they are very great. But the Giver is more precious than all His gifts."[14]

Give Jesus everything and take nothing back.

"Let us love Him, then, dear Sister, with all our might and strength. Let us belong to Him without reserve, because He wants all or nothing. And after we have once given Him everything, let us take nothing back."[15]

Allow your heart to be transformed by Christ.

"May the sacred fire consume our hearts unhindered and make of them thrones worthy of a holy love."[16]

Prayer Prompt: Dedication to the Sacred Heart

Find a quiet place and rest in the presence of Jesus. Feel free to write in your prayer journal any thoughts that arise through this prayer exercise.

Today you have an opportunity to offer yourself to the Sacred Heart of Jesus, the fount of all blessings. He is worthy of our adoration and worthy to be welcomed into our homes. (For more information about how to make an enthronement of the Sacred Heart, go to www.welcomehisheart.com.)

The Lord wants us to turn to him for all our needs, including assistance at our final moments. May we not fear our death or any challenges of our present life, but rather trust Jesus and seek a meaningful relationship with him, rooted in the sacraments and Christian love.

When you are ready, offer this prayer to the Sacred Heart of Jesus:

> Lord, I don't want to lose sight of you in my life. Help me to seek your daily protection and grow to realize the great spiritual battle that takes place around me. Cover me with your protection and keep me focused on loving you.

Let us close with this powerful prayer to the Sacred Heart of Jesus, titled "Prayer for Myself."

> O most holy Heart of Jesus, fountain of every blessing, I adore you, I love you, and with a lively sorrow for my sins, I offer you this poor heart of mine. Make me humble, patient, pure, and wholly obedient to your will. Grant, good Jesus, that I may live in you and for you. Protect me in the midst of danger; comfort me in my afflictions; give me health of body, assistance in my temporal needs, your blessings on all that I do, and the grace of a holy death. Amen.[17]

As you offer yourself to Jesus, ask him to show you how you can grow in humility, in patience, in purity, and in obedience. What does God's will in your life look like? What is he calling you to let go of so you can grow? Record your thoughts in your prayer journal.

CHAPTER 7

Pray with Me!
Personal and Traditional Prayers for Journaling and Reflection

Michele and Emily

This final chapter is designed to help you continue your journey as a woman of prayer with meditations, reflections, and prayer journaling space. We've also included some of our favorite prayers and prayers we've mentioned in earlier chapters.

Getting Started

In this section, write down your personal favorites—the things you are grateful for, your favorite titles of God, your favorite saints, and so on. These can become a point of inspiration when you need to "prime the pump" of prayer and fill your heart with hope.

Blessings from Above: Thank you, Lord, for . . .

Favorite Titles of the Lord: We worship you, Lord . . .

Prayers from the Heart: I love you, Lord, because . . .

Favorite Saints and Angels: Pray for us . . .

Intentions That We Carry on Our Heart: Dear Lord, hear us . . .

Ten Personal Reflections

The following are ten personal reflections that we've written to help you open your heart to God and express to him all you have going on in your life. Use the space provided to add your thoughts and details that fit your own situation.

Reflection One:
Calm My Inner Chaos and Bring Peace

"Peace I leave with you; my peace I give to you" (Jn 14:27).

My head is spinning with all that I need to do. I am not at peace, although I believe Christ can bring me peace. I desire his heavenly calm. I want my mind to rest, and I long to trust Christ with everything!

"My heart is restless until it rests in you," said St. Augustine. My prayer calls out to heaven as I sit at a stoplight surrounded by noise: traffic, my car, the radio blaring, and the echoes in my mind. I desire God's peace that surpasses all understanding.

Jesus whispers, "What is preventing you from resting? Why is there chaos in your soul?"

Spend some time reflecting on the word peace. . . . *Do you want it? What does it look like in your life circumstance?*

Reflection Two:
Refresh My Soul

"Whoever drinks the water I shall give will never thirst; the water I shall give will become in him a spring of water welling up to eternal life" (Jn 4:14).

Lord, show me your face. Give me a new perspective. I want to be renewed in my love for you. My life is so full and yet not of you. I want to hold your living waters within me. Cleanse me and fill me with your living waters.

You gave the woman at the well eternal water. I want that too! I want to have eternal life. You call me by name and offer me food and drink that leads to eternal life.

Lord, I want this living water to be in my soul. How can I make room for this living water in my life?

Reflection Three:
Use Me, Lord

"Be a vessel for lofty use, dedicated, beneficial to the master . . . ready for every good work" (2 Tm 2:21).

I want to be holy, Lord. I want to do your will. I want you, Christ, to use me, a broken sinner, to touch others.

I desire to be part of your kingdom. Show me the way, Lord. The more I seek to know you, the more I am aware of my weakness. Let me use my broken and weak self to bring you glory.

I need to be there for the people you want me to serve today. Lord, help me to see the people you want me to minister to. Help me to love them and share with them the spiritual blessings you have bestowed upon me. Allow me to be your hands and feet.

So many people need me, Lord. I want to share with my friends and family this gift of my faith, yet I need your grace to do so. I am weak, scared, broken. . . . I pray for these friends, family members, colleagues, neighbors, and classmates.

Whom do you want me to serve with your love?

Reflection Four:
Help Me to Be Merciful

"Be merciful, just as [also] your Father is merciful" (Lk 6:36).

It is not always easy to show mercy to others. So often I struggle to show mercy for anyone but myself. Help me, Lord, to extend mercy to everyone, even those who have "trespassed against *me.*"

Show me, Lord. Who are the people that I need to forgive, serve, and love? Help me to forgive those people and ask for forgiveness from those I have offended.

Lord, open my heart and reveal the pain hidden there. Whom do I need to forgive? Who has stomped on my heart, crushed my spirit, left me feeling abandoned and broken? Only you can mend my heart and give me grace to forgive.

Reflection Five:
Help Me to Love You above All

"[Jesus] said to him, 'You shall love the Lord, your God, with all your heart, with all your soul, and with all your mind'" (Mt 22:37).

We women love things—gadgets, clothes, shoes, bags, cars, jewelry, fashionable items, brand-new kitchens, Pinterest, decorations.

Yet, Lord, we want to love *you* above these things. We want to be detached and to surrender our "likes" of this world to you. We want to fill our hearts with gratitude for the many things you have graciously blessed us with, and make you king of everything in our lives. Teach us how to love you above all the things of this world.

It is so easy to get wrapped up in the things of this world. Lord, what things do I need to relinquish so that I can cling to you alone? What is distracting me from you?

Reflection Six:
Beautiful in the Eyes of the Lord

"How beautiful you are, my friend, how beautiful you are!" (Sg 4:1).

Lord, I often feel as though I am not enough: not good enough, not holy enough, not special enough. Help me to know that I am everything to you. Let me sit before the refiner's fire: mold me into the woman you want me to be.

Hear Jesus speaking: "You are beautiful, my child, come rest in me. I am your hiding place, your fortress, your stronghold. I wait for you each day to come to me. Talk to me, tell me the desires of your heart. In me you will find your strength; in me you will know you are not lacking. See your reflection in my eyes, and know the treasure I have made in you. I love you."

What is Jesus whispering to your heart? Can you feel his loving gaze?

Reflection Seven:
When I Am Suffering

"Our hope for you is firm, for we know that as you share in the sufferings, you also share in the encouragement" (2 Cor 1:7).

Lord, my heart is so sad and broken right now. I come before you in my deepest sorrow. I have nothing to bring to you but my pain. Please do not abandon me, Jesus. Help me to feel your presence. I do not understand this trial, Jesus; help me to trust in you. Help me to know your love.

Look at a crucifix. Hear Jesus speak to you: "I love you . . . I love you so much I died on the Cross for you." How does this make you feel?

Reflection Eight:
When I Am Afraid

"Be strong and steadfast; have no fear . . . for it is the LORD, your God, who marches with you; he will never fail you or forsake you" (Dt 31:6).

Jesus, I am so alone and scared. The storms of life rage against me, and I feel that I am losing all hope. Jesus, I feel like the disciples on the boat in the storm, and as they did, I ask, "Do you not care?" (Mk 4:38).

Yet I know you have not abandoned me. You respond to me as you did to those on the boat, "Why are you terrified?" (Mk 4:40).

Jesus, help me to reach for your hand and walk side by side with you in the sea of life. Guide me and direct me. I don't want to fear these difficult moments. Instead, I desire to trust you and develop a personal relationship with you.

Picture yourself in a fishing boat with Jesus. The water is calm, and the boat is serenely floating on the water. Tell Jesus about your greatest fears. Can you feel his presence?

Reflection Nine:
When I Am Anxious

"Cast all your worries upon him because he cares for you" (1 Pt 5:7).

Lord, the future is full of unknowns and can feel overwhelming. When I start to think about tomorrow, I often lose track of today and the graces you offer me now. Jesus, I know I cannot do this with my own strength.

Shield me, protect me, and turn my eyes from the darkness to see you as the light. Allow me to see your plan and purpose for me. Help me to cast my anxiety at the foot of the Cross and cling to you. May your peace wash over me and take away my uncertainties.

Imagine you are standing under a waterfall and Jesus is washing away all your anxiety. What do you give to him? How does this make you feel?

Reflection Ten:
Praying at the Foot of the Cross

Visio divina allows you to contemplate God through sacred images. Use the image below as a focal point and gaze upon it.[1]

Place yourself in God's presence and take a few deep breaths. Then read the following passage slowly, noticing the words and phrases that draw your attention.

> Standing by the cross of Jesus were his mother and his mother's sister, Mary the wife of Clopas, and Mary of Magdala. When Jesus saw his mother and the disciple there whom he loved, he said to his mother, "Woman, behold, your son." Then he said to the disciple, "Behold, your mother." And from that hour the disciple took her into his home. (Jn 19:25–27)

Gaze upon the image of Mary at the foot of the Cross. What strikes you about this image?

Gaze upon the image again and spend a moment in silence. What do you see this time? How is God speaking to you?

Gaze upon the image a third time and spend a moment in silence. Allow God to lead you in prayer. Journal your prayer here:

Close with a prayer of thanksgiving. Offer a simple prayer such as, "Dear Lord, thank you for this time we spent together meditating on your gift of the Blessed Mother to us. Thank you for her example of faith-filled suffering. May she lead us more closely to you."

My Prayer Journal, Chapter by Chapter

Below is a place for you to reflect more deeply on the questions raised in the first six chapters of this book. Record your thoughts here or in a separate journal. The purpose of this is to help you go deeper, and to hear more clearly what God is trying to teach you through this book.

Chapter 1
The Power of Prayer: A Holy Invitation

- From "Do You Have Time for God?" (pages 7–9).

    ◊ Is there a part of Angel's story that resonates with you?
    ◊ When was the last time God had your full attention?

- From "Let's Pray: Rest in Jesus' Presence" (pages 9–10).

    ◊ Tell Jesus what is on your mind.
    ◊ Have you ever heard God speak to you?

- From "Meet Your Heavenly Friend: St. Gemma Galgani" (pages 10–12).

    ◊ St. Gemma's story reminds us that the path to sanctity often involves following in the footsteps of the saints and asking for their intercession. Which saints do you most admire and why?
    ◊ What have you learned from their lives, writings, and prayers?

- From "Prayer Prompt: Talk to Jesus" (pages 13–14). Think of Jesus as he appears in your favorite Gospel story. Place yourself in his presence, and then:
  ◊ Tell Jesus what is on your heart—your hopes, your fears, what you experienced today.
  ◊ What are some of the things for which you are most grateful?
  ◊ Sit in silence, and let Jesus speak to your heart. Ask him to reveal his will for your life. What did you hear? What would you most like to receive from him today?

Chapter 2
The Basics of Prayer: Seek Him, Ask Him, Discover Him

- From "'Adulting' in Prayer" (pages 16–19).
  ◊ How would you describe your relationship with God?
  ◊ How do you seek, ask, and discover God?
  ◊ How has your relationship with God changed over time?

- From "Love Notes from God" (pages 19–21).
  ◊ When was the last time you received a "love note" from God?
  ◊ Read Matthew 14:22–23. What is Jesus saying to you? Can you hear him calling you much like he called Peter?
  ◊ Are there storms raging in your life? How will you step out of the boat?

- From "Build a Prayer Plan" (pages 21–25).
  - ◊ What is your prayer plan?
  - ◊ When and where can you spend daily time with God, just the two of you?
  - ◊ How can you begin to make that a priority?

- From "Let's Pray: Lectio Divina" (pages 25–26).
  - ◊ As you follow the guided meditation, record your thoughts and impressions.

- From "Prayer Prompt: The Our Father" (pages 30–31).
  - ◊ Share with Jesus how you feel about the Our Father. What parts of the prayer do you struggle with?
  - ◊ Is there someone you need to forgive right now?
  - ◊ As you pray the Our Father slowly, focusing on each word, what phrases jump out at you and speak to your heart?

Chapter 3
Living Pray-Fully: Praying through the Day

- From "Michele's Introduction" (pages 33–40).
  - ◊ What's on your mind today?
  - ◊ As you sit quietly in God's presence and scattered thoughts cross your mind, jot them down—then set them mentally aside. Bring yourself gently back to sitting with Jesus. Don't let anything come between you.

- From "Prayer Prompt: Make an Examen" (pages 44–46).
  - ◊ How do you see God?
  - ◊ For what are you grateful?
  - ◊ Write a prayer to the Holy Spirit.
  - ◊ What do you regret about today?
  - ◊ Write a prayer of sorrow and forgiveness.
  - ◊ What is your resolution for tomorrow?

Chapter 4
Becoming Women of Prayer: Cultivating a Legacy of Prayerfulness

- From "Five Things I Learned from My Family About Prayer" (pages 49–53).
  - ◊ Who are the people in your family who have been the greatest influence on your spiritual life?
  - ◊ What did they do that made an impression on you?

- From "The Gift of Spiritual Community" (pages 53–54).
  - ◊ Who are the spiritual friends who have meant the most to you, and why?
  - ◊ Where do you find a community of support to help you grow in your faith?

- From "Let's Pray: Love One Another" (page 55).
  - ◊ Who needs you to show them love the most in their life right now? How can you do that best?

◊ How can you continue the legacy of faith in your own family or greater community?

- From "Prayer Prompt: Pray for a Legacy of Faith" (pages 59–60).

    ◊ Who has inspired you to become a stronger woman of prayer? How can you pass on a legacy of prayer to others?

    ◊ Write a prayer asking Jesus to help you in the specific areas of your life where you feel you most need to cultivate courage.

    ◊ Read again John 14:27. What strikes you about this "peace passage"?

Chapter 5
Hello, Is Anyone Listening? The Mystery of Unanswered Prayer

- From "Ask and You Shall Receive?" (pages 64–67).

    ◊ Can you remember a time when you asked but did not receive what you wanted? Did any good come out of this unanswered prayer?

    ◊ Reread Luke 24:26. How have you experienced the truth of this passage in your life?

- From "Let's Pray: Remember God's Goodness" (page 67).

    ◊ Can you think of a time God answered a prayer for you? Write a prayer of gratitude in response.

◊ Remember a time when it seemed your prayers were not answered. How did you feel?

◊ Did God answer your prayer in an unexpected way, or reveal himself to you in your difficulty? If you cannot see God's hand during this time, ask him to show you.

- From "Prayer Prompt: 'I Am Always in Your Midst'" (pages 72–73). Reread the poem. Then respond to the following:

◊ Which words spoke to you?

◊ Do you believe you are a beautiful work of art created by God? How does that make you feel?

◊ Write a poem or letter to God in response to reading this poem and the questions that follow on page 73.

Chapter 6
Prayer Protections: Devotions to Draw Us Deeper into Prayer

- From "Let's Pray: Visio Divina" (pages 79–81).

◊ As you contemplate the image on page 80 and ponder the scripture passage (Rom 8:38–39), record your thoughts and impressions.

- From "Prayer Prompt: Dedication to the Sacred Heart" (pages 85–86).

◊ As you offer yourself to Jesus, ask him to show you how you can grow in humility, in patience, in purity, and in obedience.

◊ What does God's will in your life look like?
◊ What is he calling you to let go of (or take up) so you
   can grow?

Our Favorite Prayers

In this final section of chapter 7, we want to share with you some of our favorite traditional prayers. As you offer them, use the lectio divina technique (see page 25) to dig deeper and meditate on the words, so that they might become a "prayer starter" you can use to express your own thoughts to God.

At the end of this section you will find a place to record your own favorite prayers, to keep them handy for when you need them most.

Novena to St. Margaret Mary Alacoque

O St. Margaret Mary, through you, Jesus pours out his abundant graces on all mankind. Help us to put aside our personal interests and abandon ourselves entirely and lovingly to his adorable heart. May our work, like yours, merit his special care and favor, through Jesus' Holy Name.

St. Margaret Mary, we implore you, to whom the Sacred Heart of Jesus manifested his divine treasures, to obtain the graces we seek from his adorable heart. With unlimited confidence, we ask: (*Share your request.*)

O Glorious St. Margaret Mary, through your intercession, may the Divine Heart of Jesus continue to be glorified and loved.

Say: Our Father . . . Hail Mary . . . Glory Be . . .

(Pray for nine days in succession)

Today I offer this novena for the following intention:

The Miracle Prayer
Fr. Peter Mary Rookey

From Fr. Rookey: "Say this prayer faithfully, no matter what you feel. When you come to the point where you sincerely mean each word with all your heart, something good spiritually will happen to you. You will experience Jesus, and he will change your whole life in a very special way. You will see."

Lord Jesus, I come before you just as I am. I am sorry for my sins; I repent of my sins; please forgive me. In your name I forgive all others for what they have done against me. I renounce Satan, the evil spirits, and all their works. I give you my entire self, Lord Jesus, now and forever.

I invite you into my life, Jesus. I accept you as my Lord, God, and Savior. Heal me, change me, strengthen me in body, soul, and spirit. Come, Lord Jesus, cover me with your Precious Blood, and fill me with your Holy Spirit. I love you, Lord Jesus. I praise you, Jesus. I thank you, Jesus. I shall follow you every day of my life. Amen.

Mary, Mother of Sorrows, Queen of Peace, St. Peregrine, the cancer saint, all you angels and saints, please help me. Amen.

Today I offer this prayer for the following intention:

Prayer to the Sacred Heart of Jesus

O most holy Heart of Jesus, fountain of every blessing, I adore you, I love you, and with a lively sorrow for my sins, I offer you this poor heart of mine. Make me humble, patient, pure, and wholly obedient to your will. Grant, good Jesus, that I may live in you and for you. Protect me in the midst of danger; comfort me in my afflictions; give me health of body, assistance in my temporal needs, your blessings on all that I do, and the grace of a holy death. Amen.[2]

Today I offer this prayer for the following intention:

Rosary of Abandonment
Fr. Dolindo Ruotolo

*Many of us are plagued by anxiety and fear. The Rosary of Aban-
donment is an opportunity to pause for a few moments and give all
of our worries to Jesus and allow Mary, his mother, to guide us. As
you pray these words, try breathing deeply with each "Jesus, you
take over!" or "Mother Mary, guide me." Imagine Jesus and Mary
comforting you and taking away all your burdens.*

God, come to my assistance.
Lord, make haste to help me.
> *Say a Glory Be, an Our Father, and a Hail Mary.*

- 1st Decade: Jesus, you take over! (*Repeat 10 times*)
  Glory Be . . .

- 2nd Decade: Mother Mary, guide me. (*Repeat 10 times*)
  Glory Be . . .

- 3rd Decade: Jesus, you take over! (*Repeat 10 times*)
  Glory Be . . .

- 4th Decade: Mother Mary, guide me. (*Repeat 10 times*)
  Glory Be . . .

- 5th Decade: Jesus, you take over! (*Repeat 10 times*)
  Glory Be . . .
  (In conclusion:) Hail Holy Queen . . .
  Today I offer this prayer for the following intention:

My Favorite Prayers

My Favorite Prayers

My Favorite Prayers

My Favorite Prayers

Study Guide

1. The Power of Prayer: A Holy Invitation

1. What was your primary takeaway from this chapter?
2. This chapter shares the miraculous story of Angel's healing from cancer. Have you had a time in your life when God answered a prayer in a powerful way?
3. What are some of the biggest obstacles to prayer that you face?
4. Bishop Cullinan gave some advice on talking to Jesus and how we can experience him in our daily lives (see page 9). Have you ever felt Jesus in your day? Give an example.
5. The saints give us a holy example of how to live prayerfully. What struck you about the life of St. Gemma Galgani? Which piece of advice from her spoke to you the most?

2. The Basics of Prayer: Seek Him, Ask Him, Discover Him

1. What was your primary takeaway from this chapter?
2. What type of prayers do you typically say? Do you find yourself praying only for blessings and for things you want or need? Could you relate to Emily's life raft analogy?
3. How can you expand your prayer life? Do you take time out to pray daily and meditate on the life of Christ?
4. How can prayer fuel your works as it did for Mother Teresa? Do you think she could have accomplished all that she did without prayer?
5. Have you ever felt called to perform an act of mercy or love because of an inspiration through prayer?

3. Living Pray-Fully: Praying through the Day

1. What was your primary takeaway from this chapter?
2. In this chapter Michele shares how she heard an answer to her prayer through the radio. Have you ever heard God speak to you through others, the media, scripture, or spiritual reading?
3. What things can you cut out of your day that would make more time for prayer?
4. Which of the ways mentioned in this chapter can help you integrate prayer into your daily life?
5. St. Gianna Beretta Molla was a modern-day woman, wife, mother, and physician who gave the ultimate sacrifice of her life for her child. What struck you most about her story? Which piece of advice from her spoke to you?

4. Becoming Women of Prayer: Cultivating a Legacy of Prayerfulness

1. What was your primary takeaway from this chapter?
2. Have you ever been aware of someone praying for you as you made an important decision in your life? Who has greatly influenced your faith life for the better? Parents? Siblings? Friends?
3. Have you ever prayed a novena that was answered in an unexpected way like the red roses on the side of the road? If so, what happened?
4. What are some examples of practices or positive influences from others that have helped you grow deeper in your faith? Attending Catholic school? Retreats? Youth gatherings? Prayer groups?
5. Have you ever heard of St. Zélie? Did you find her relatable?

5. Hello, Is Anyone Listening?: The Mystery of Unanswered Prayer

1. What was your primary takeaway from this chapter?
2. The loss of her husband led Rose to a new understanding of prayer and to see God's presence in her life, even when times were difficult. Have you ever experienced your prayers answered in a different way than you asked but a way that led you deeper into relationship with God?
3. Do you see prayer as an anchor in your life that helps you through challenging times? Have you ever experienced the power of prayer and peace of God when going through a difficulty?
4. In this chapter, we shared the story of Fr. Jim Willig's dialogue with Jesus when he was angry and suffering with cancer. He opened up to Jesus in prayer in a way he never thought he could. Do you feel like you can share openly with Jesus, even when you are angry? Have you ever experienced this?
5. St. Edith Stein was a modern-day mystic, philosopher, and martyr. What struck you most about her story? Which piece of advice from her spoke to you most?

6. Prayer Protections: Devotions to Draw Us Deeper into Prayer

1. What was your primary takeaway from this chapter?
2. Have you ever heard of enthronement of the Sacred Heart? Have you ever dedicated your life to Jesus or Mary in a special way outside of Baptism?
3. What does "spiritual protection" mean to you? Do you seek God's protection on a regular basis?

4. What is your relationship with the Rosary? Do you see a
    value in this type of meditative prayer for growing closer
    to Christ?
5. Have you ever heard of St. Margaret Mary? What struck
    you most about her story?

Acknowledgments

Permission is gratefully acknowledged to cite from the following works:

Permission to quote excerpts from *Essays on Woman* by Edith Stein translated by Freda Mary Oben, PhD. Copyright © 1987, 1996 is granted from Washington Province of Discalced Carmelites, ICS Publications, 2131 Lincoln Road, N.E., Washington, DC 20002-1199 U.S.A. www.icspublications.org.

Excerpts from *The Hidden Life* translated by Waltraut Stein, PhD. Copyright © 1992 reprinted by permission of Washington Province of Discalced Carmelites, ICS Publication, 2131 Lincoln Road, N.E., Washington, DC 20002-1199 U.S.A. www.icspublications.org.

"Sacred Heart of Jesus." Copyrighted Classic Image by Adolfo Simeone used by permission from Cromo NB Italy. www.cromo.com.

"At the Foot of the Cross." Image credit Bernadette Carstensen, 2014. Used with permission, Columbus Catholic Women's Conference.

"Miracle Prayer" by Fr. Peter Rookey © 1993, Servite Fathers, O.S.M. Reprinted with permission of the Servite Fathers.

Notes

Introduction: Why Is Prayer Important?

1. Michael J. Denk, *Pray 40 Days* (Cleveland, OH: Prodigal Father Publishing, 2018), 21.

2. The same study reported that 20 percent pray once a week, 14 percent pray less than weekly, and less than 10 percent pray a few times a year. Mark M. Grary and Mary L. Gautier, "Catholic Women in the United States," Center for Applied Research in the Apostolate, accessed April 18, 2019, https://cara.georgetown.edu/CatholicWomenStudy.pdf, 5–6.

3. "Pope Francis: Prayer Opens the Door for God," October 8, 2013, Vatican Radio, accessed April 18, 2019, http://www.archivioradiovaticana.va/storico/2013/10/08/pope_francis_prayer_opens_the_door_for_god_/in2-735421.

1. The Power of Prayer: A Holy Invitation

1. "Consolation for Angel Fox," February 7, 2017, *From the Chair*, St. Gabriel Catholic Radio, https://stgabrielradio.com/02-07-17-from-the-chair-bishop-campbell-consolation-for-angel-fox/.

2. Michele Faehnle and Emily Jaminet, *The Friendship Project: The Catholic Woman's Guide to Making and Keeping Fabulous, Faith-Filled Friends* (Notre Dame, IN: Ave Maria Press, 2017), xi.

3. John Bartunek, *The Better Part: A Christ-Centered Resource for Personal Prayer* (Clayton, NC: Ministry23, 2014), 644.

4. Alphonsus Cullinan, Homily, Dublin Irish Festival Mass, August 5, 2017.

5. Amedeo, C.P., "Biography of St. Gemma Galgani," trans. Osmund Thorpe, C.P., St. Gemma Galgani (website), accessed April 18, 2019, http://www.stgemmagalgani.com/p/blessed-gemma-galgani-biography-of.html.

6. "A Prayer before Confession by St. Gemma Galgani," Our Catholic Prayers, accessed April 18, 2019, https://www.ourcatholicprayers.com/st-gemma-before-confession.html.

7. All the "advice" quotes in this section are from "Quotes of St. Gemma Galgani," St. Gemma Galgani (website), accessed April 18, 2019, http://www.stgemmagalgani.com/.

8. "A Prayer before Confession by St. Gemma Galgani."

2. The Basics of Prayer: Seek Him, Ask Him, Discover Him

1. Bartunek, *The Better Part*, 18.

2. Ralph Martin, *The Fulfillment of All Desire: A Guidebook for the Journey to God Based on the Wisdom of the Saints* (Steubenville: Emmaus Road Pub., 2006), 31.

3. Margaret Mary Alacoque, *The Letters of St. Margaret Mary Alacoque, Apostle of the Sacred Heart* (Rockford: Tan Books, 1997), 32.

4. Bartunek, *The Better Part*, 6–49.

5. Francis de Sales, *Introduction to the Devout Life* (New York: Vintage Books, 2002), 47.

6. Martin, *The Fulfillment of All Desire*, 284.

7. Brian Kolodiejchuk, M.C., "A Joyful Witness to Mercy," September 1, 2016, Knights of Columbus (website), www.kofc.org/en/columbia/detail/joyful-witness-mercy.html.

8. Leo Maasburg, *Mother Teresa of Calcutta: A Personal Portrait*, trans. Michael J. Miller (San Francisco: Ignatius Press, 2011), 80.

9. From the official website of the Mother Teresa of Calcutta Center, Contemplative Sisters, accessed April 2019, www.motherteresa.org/contemplative-sisters.html.

10. Susan Conroy, *Praying with Mother Teresa* (Stockbridge, MA: Marian Press, 2016), 177.

11. Conroy, *Praying with Mother Teresa*, 21.

12. Conroy, *Praying with Mother Teresa*, 20.

13. Conroy, *Praying with Mother Teresa*, 21.

14. Conroy, *Praying with Mother Teresa*, 103.

15. Maasburg, *Mother Teresa of Calcutta*, 90.

16. "Mother Teresa," Missionaries of Charity Fathers (website), accessed April 28, 2019, http://www.mcfathers.org/mother-teresa.html.

3. Living Pray-Fully: Praying through the Day

1. Michael E. Gaitley, M.I.C., *Consoling the Heart of Jesus: A Do-It-Yourself Retreat, Inspired by the Spiritual Exercises of St. Ignatius* (Stockbridge, MA: Marian Press, 2010), 33.

2. Francis de Sales, *Introduction to the Devout Life*, 48.

3. Bartunek, *The Better Part*, 10.

4. Denk, *Pray 40 Days*, 17.

5. Maria Faustina Kowalska, *Diary: Divine Mercy in My Soul* (Stockbridge, MA: Marian Press, 1987), 164.

6. Don Pickrell, "How Much Time Do Americans Spend behind the Wheel?" December 9, 2017, Volpe National Transportation Systems Center, accessed April 18, 2019, https://www.volpe.dot.gov/news/how-much-time-do-americans-spend-behind-wheel.

7. John Paul II, "Address to Young People of Bologna," September 27, 1997, Libreria Editrice Vaticana, accessed April 19, 2019, https://w2.vatican.

va/content/john-paul-ii/en/speeches/1997/september/documents/hf_
jp-ii_spe_19970927_youth-bologna.html.

    8. John Riccardo, *Heaven Starts Now: Becoming a Saint Day by Day* (Frederick, MD: Word Among Us Press, 2016), 14.

    9. John Paul II, "On the Mystery and Worship of the Eucharist," February 24, 1980, Libreria Editrice Vaticana, accessed August 9, 2019, https://
w2.vatican.va/content/john-paul-ii/en/letters/1980/documents/hf_jp-ii_
let_19800224_dominicae-cenae.html.

    10. Gianna Beretta Molla, *Love Letters to My Husband*, ed. Elio Guerriero (Boston: Pauline Books & Media, 2002), 3.

    11. "Catholic Action," n.d., Saint Gianna Beretta Molla (website), accessed April 19, 2019, https://saintgianna.org/catholic.htm.

    12. "Homily of John Paul II: Canonization of Six New Saints," May 16, 2004, Libreria Editrice Vaticana, accessed April 19, 2019, http://w2.vatican.va/content/john-paul-ii/en/homilies/2004/documents/hf_jp-ii_
hom_20040516_canonizations.html.

    13. "Catholic Action."

    14. Molla, *Love Letters to My Husband*, 27.

    15. Molla, *Love Letters to My Husband*, 28.

    16. Molla, *Love Letters to My Husband*, 40.

    17. Molla, *Love Letters to My Husband*, 46.

    18. Molla, *Love Letters to My Husband*, 80.

4. Becoming Women of Prayer: Cultivating a Legacy of Prayerfulness

    1. John Paul II, apostolic letter *Novo Millennio Ineunte*, January 6, 2001, Section 33, Libreria Editrice Vaticana, w2.vatican.va/content/john-paul-ii/
en/apost_letters/2001/documents/hf_jp-ii_apl_20010106_novo-millennio-ineunte.html.

    2. Kieran Kavanaugh, O.C.D., and Otilio Rodriguez, trans., *The Collected Works of St. Teresa of Avila*, vol. 1 (Washington, DC: ICS Publications, 1976), 64–65.

    3. Genevieve of the Holy Face, *The Mother of the Little Flower: Zélie Martin, 1831–1877* (Chicago: Tan Books, 2005).

    4. Program for Canonization Ceremony for Sts. Louis and Zélie Martin, October 18, 2015, http://www.vatican.va/news_services/liturgy/libretti/2015/20151018-libretto-canonizzazione.pdf.

    5. "Louis and Zelie Martin," Society of the Little Flower (website), accessed March 15, 2018, www.littleflower.org/therese/life-story/
her-parents/.

    6. "Louis and Zelie Martin."

    7. Genevieve of the Holy Face, *The Mother of the Little Flower*, 2.

    8. Genevieve of the Holy Face, *The Mother of the Little Flower*, 3.

9. Zélie and Louis Martin, *A Call to a Deeper Love: The Family Correspondence of the Parents of St. Thérèse of the Child Jesus, 1863–1885*, trans. Ann Connors Hess (New York: Society of St. Paul, 2011), 28.

10. Martin and Martin, *A Call to a Deeper Love*, 88.

11. Martin and Martin, *A Call to a Deeper Love*, 346.

12. Genevieve of the Holy Face, *The Mother of the Little Flower*, 10.

13. Martin and Martin, *A Call to a Deeper Love*, 139.

14. Martin and Martin, *A Call to a Deeper Love*, 10.

5. Hello, Is Anyone Listening?: The Mystery of Unanswered Prayer

1. Jim Willig with Tammy Bundy, *Lessons from the School of Suffering: A Young Priest with Cancer Teaches Us How to Live* (Cincinnati: St. Anthony Messenger Press, 2001), 59.

2. Willig and Bundy, *Lessons from the School of Suffering*, 61.

3. Jacques Philippe, *Nine Days to Rediscover the Joy of Prayer* (New York: Scepter Publishers, 2019), 85.

4. *Life in a Jewish Family: Edith Stein: An Autobiography, 1891–1916*, trans. Josephine Koeppel, O.C.D. (Washington, DC: ICS Publications, 2016), 278.

5. Waltraud Herbstrith, *Edith Stein, a Biography*, trans. Fr. Bernard Bonowitz (San Francisco: Ignatius Press, 1992), 101.

6. Elizabeth A. Mitchell, Prudence Allen, and Terrence C. Wright, *Edith Stein: Seeker of Truth* (Denver, CO: Endow, 2008).

7. "Teresa Benedict of the Cross: Edith Stein (1891–1942)," Vatican website, accessed June 27, 2019, http://www.vatican.va/news_services/liturgy/saints/ns_lit_doc_19981011_edith_stein_en.html.

8. "Teresa Benedict of the Cross: Edith Stein (1891–1942)."

9. Edith Stein, *Self-Portrait in Letters, 1916–1942*, trans. Josephine Koeppel, O.C.D. (Washington, DC: ICS Publications, 1993), 45, 54.

10. Edith Stein, *Essays on Woman*, trans. Freda Mary Oben, ed. Lucy Gelber and Romaeus Leuven (Washington, DC: ICS Publications, 2017), 143–45.

11. Stein, *Essays on Woman*, 144.

12. Stein, *Essays on Woman*, 145.

13. Edith Stein, *Das Weihnachtsgeheimnis*, in *Wege zur inneren Stille*, ed. W. Herbstrith (Frankfurt: Kaffke Verlag, 1978), 22–23.

14. L. Gerber and Michael Linssin, eds., *The Collected Works of Edith Stein*, vol. 4: *The Hidden Life: Essays, Meditations, Spiritual Texts*, trans. Waltraut Stein (Washington, DC: ICS Publications, 2014), section IV.4.2.

6. Prayer Protections: Devotions to Draw Us Deeper into Prayer

1. Francis Larkin, *Enthronement of the Sacred Heart* (Boston: Daughters of St. Paul, 1978), 12.

2. Larkin, *Enthronement of the Sacred Heart*, 17.

3. Larkin, *Enthronement of the Sacred Heart*, 12.

4. "Popular Devotional Practices: Basic Questions and Answers," November 12, 2003, United States Conference of Catholic Bishops (website), accessed April 20, 2019, http://www.usccb.org/prayer-and-worship/prayers-and-devotions/prayers/popular-devotional-practices-basic-questions-and-answers.cfm.

5. Pius XII, encyclical letter *On the Sacred Liturgy* (*Mediator Dei*), November 20, 1947, Libreria Editrice Vaticana, accessed April 2019, http://w2.vatican.va/content/pius-xii/en/encyclicals/documents/hf_p-xii_enc_20111947_mediator-dei.html.

6. "Sacred Heart of Jesus." Copyrighted Classic Image by Adolfo Simeone. Used by permission from Cromo NB Italy.

7. Kathleen Beckman, "Marian Consecration: Protection from Sin and Evil," quoting the Thirteenth Ordinary General Assembly of the Synod of Bishops, October 26, 2012, accessed August 13, 2019, Catholic Exchange, https://catholicexchange.com/marian-consecration-protection-from-sin-and-evil.

8. Joseph Pronechen, "15 Super Promises of Our Blessed Mother for Faithfully Praying the Rosary," National Catholic Register, October 15, 2015, www.ncregister.com/blog/joseph-pronechen/15-super-promises-of-our-blessed-mother-for-faithfully-praying-the-rosary.

9. Edward Sri, *Praying the Rosary like Never Before*, https://blog.franciscanmedia.org/franciscan-spirit/why-pray-the-rosary.

10. Alacoque, *The Letters,* VII.

11. Alacoque, *The Letters,* VII.

12. Alacoque, *The Letters,* VII.

13. Portions of the biography of St. Margaret Mary Alacoque were first printed at Catholic Digest.com on October 16, 2018. Reprinted with permission.

14. Alacoque, *The Letters,* VII. St. Margaret Mary to Mother de Saumaise, 1682.

15. Alacoque, *The Letters,* VII. St. Margaret Mary to Sister Felice-Madeleine, 1686.

16. Margaret Mary letter to Mother de Saumaise, at Dijon, July 10, 1673.

17. Francis Larkin, *Enthronement of the Sacred Heart* (Boston, MA: Daughters of St. Paul, 1978), 541.

7. Pray with Me!: Personal and Traditional Prayers for Journaling and Reflection

1. Image copyright Columbus Catholic Women's Conference, used with permission. Bernadette Carstensen, 2014, all rights reserved.

2. Larkin, *Enthronement of the Sacred Heart*, 491.

My Journal

My Journal

My Journal

My Journal

My Journal

My Journal

My Journal

My Journal

My Journal

My Journal

My Journal

My Journal

My Journal

Michele Faehnle is a school nurse at St. Andrew School in Upper Arlington, Ohio, and the host of *Answering the Call* on St. Gabriel Radio. She is a contributor to CatholicMom.com, codirector of the Columbus Catholic Women's Conference, and coauthor of *Divine Mercy for Moms*, *The Friendship Project*, and *Our Friend Faustina*.

Faehnle earned a bachelor of science degree in nursing from Franciscan University of Steubenville in 1999 and is working toward licensing as a school nurse. Faehnle has spoken at the National Shrine of Divine Mercy and to several women's groups and conferences, including 1:38 Women, Mothering with Grace Annual Mother's Conference, Indiana Catholic Women's Conference, and the online Catholic Conference for Moms. Faehnle has appeared on EWTN's *At Home with Jim and Joy* and a number of Catholic radio programs.

Along with her coauthor, Emily Jaminet, Faehnle received the Bishop John King Mussio Award from Franciscan University of Steubenvile, of which she is an alumna. She and her husband, Matthew, have four children and live in Columbus, Ohio.

Emily Jaminet is executive director of the Sacred Heart Enthronement Network, a contributor to CatholicMom.com, and coauthor of *Divine Mercy for Moms*, *The Friendship Project*, and *Our Friend Faustina*. She serves on the board of directors of the Columbus Catholic Women's Conference. Jaminet earned a bachelor's degree in mental health and human services from Franciscan University of Steubenville in 1998.

Jaminet offers a daily segment called *A Mother's Moment* on St. Gabriel Catholic Radio and Mater Dei Radio. She has spoken to several women's groups and conferences, including 1:38 Women, Mothering with Grace Annual Mother's Conference, Indiana Catholic Women's Conference, Women's Day of Reflection for Homeschoolers, and the online Catholic Conference for Moms. Jaminet has appeared on EWTN's *At Home with Jim and Joy* and a number of Catholic radio programs.

Along with her coauthor, Michele Faehnle, Jaminet received the Bishop John King Mussio Award from Franciscan University of Steubenvile, of which she is an alumna. She and her husband, John, have seven children and live in Columbus, Ohio.

http://inspirethefaith.com
Facebook: St. Teresa's Online Book Club

ALSO BY
MICHELE FAEHNLE
AND EMILY JAMINET

Divine Mercy for Moms
**Sharing the Lessons
of St. Faustina**

The Divine Mercy devotion of St. Faustina
Kowalska is one of the most celebrated of all
Catholic devotions. In their first book, two lifelong
"friends of Faustina" break open the history,
practices, and prayers associated with this
devotion, guiding busy moms to receive God's
message of Divine Mercy and to pass it on to
others through their words, deeds, and prayers
in imitation of Mary, the Mother of Mercy.

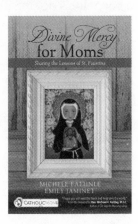

The Friendship Project
**The Catholic Woman's Guide
to Making and Keeping Fabulous,
Faith-Filled Friends**

Drawing on the cardinal and theological
virtues, stories of the saints, and anecdotes
from their own friendships, Michele Faehnle
and Emily Jaminet provide a practical primer
for any Catholic woman seeking ways to deepen
old friendships and develop new ones of virtue.

**Look for these titles wherever books and eBooks are sold.
Visit avemariapress.com for more information.**